THE SOCIAL SCIENTIST IN AMERICAN INDUSTRY

THE SOCIAL SCIENTIST
IN AMERICAN INDUSTRY

Self-Perception of Role, Motivation, and Career

MATTHEW RADOM

RUTGERS UNIVERSITY PRESS

NEW BRUNSWICK, NEW JERSEY

Copyright © 1970 by Rutgers University, the State University of New Jersey
Library of Congress Catalog Card Number: 76-125193
SBN: 8135-0665-4

Manufactured in the United States of America
by H. Wolff Book Manufacturing Company, Inc., New York, N.Y.

To Marjorie

CONTENTS

PREFACE

American industry has produced an amazing array of goods and services through technological advances in the years after World War II. Funds for industrial research and development were greatly increased, and competition for the services of highly trained scientists and engineers reached unprecedented heights. Some observers believed that the apparent shortage of these professionals was due more to under-utilization than to an actual shortage in numbers of those available for employment in corporate research laboratories. A number of important studies were undertaken involving laboratory scientists and engineers and the published results gave industrial leaders a better understanding of the special problems that arose in administering the services of these highly educated people when they became full-time employees in private enterprise.

All during this period, rapid technological growth was producing perplexing economic, social, and political problems that affected the private sector of the economy as well as the public welfare. Corporation executives found that they could no longer rely exclusively on their experiences to guide their actions. A new body of knowledge was needed to cope with the mounting problems, knowledge that involved the social sciences.

Although the number of physical scientists has steadily increased over the last decade, in percentage terms of all scientists
employed in American industry, the proportion of social scientists has doubled while that of physical scientists has remained
relatively stable. Yet, there has been no major study that has
delved into the world of work of the social scientist employed
full-time in industry. This book is an attempt to fill that void.

There are about three thousand social scientists with doctoral
degrees working in American industry. They represent about
one-sixth of all scientists with doctorates in their fields who are
employed in private enterprise. Traditionally, social scientists
with doctoral training have not been attracted to careers in
industry. In recent years, however, attitudes have changed, for
young Ph.D.s have found that industrial enterprise offered unusual opportunities for large-scale research on challenging
problems. Having embarked on a career in industry, social
scientists found, as data in this book will show, that there was
great variety as well as opportunity to use their professional
training to a very high degree.

In the chapters to follow, analysis of responses to questions
asked of a relatively large sample of industrial social scientists
about why they accepted employment in industry, what roles
they see themselves playing, and how they view their careers
should help us to understand the motivational forces at work
for highly trained professionals. It is the hope of the author
that this book will add something of value to the growing list
of the literature concerned with learning how American industry can attract and hold our most highly educated people in
self-actualizing careers.

I am greatly indebted to the many social scientists in industry
who generously gave their time to help me with this study.
Without their observations, which were always given candidly
and without hesitation, I would not have been able to mine the
rich field that was opened for me. Their cooperation was most
heartening and encouraged me to continue my research despite
the many practical problems that arose, largely of my own mak-

ing, of trying to do such an ambitious study while carrying a full teaching load.

Several social scientists whom I hold in great esteem were extremely helpful in suggesting how I could proceed with the project and avoid common pitfalls in this type of research. My old friend and mentor at Columbia University, Professor Eli Ginzberg, not only provided deep insight but also graciously allowed me to use some of the questions he and John Herma included in their study, which culminated in their book *Talent and Performance*. Donald C. Pelz and Frank M. Andrews, of the University of Michigan's Survey Research Center, very kindly gave me permission to include a number of the questions they used in their study, since published under the title *Scientists in Industry*, so that I could make direct comparisons of the responses of Ph.D. physical scientists in industry with those of my respondents in the social sciences on certain aspects of work in private enterprise. Simon Marcson, a friend and colleague at Rutgers University who has done considerable work with scientists in industry, gave generously of his time whenever I asked for his help. His book, *The Scientist in American Industry*, stands, in my opinion, as a beacon to guide other researchers in adding more light to what we should know about highly trained people in industry so that there can be more effective use of these professionals to improve our industrial society.

I owe particular thanks to Donald King and Janice Ralph of the Rutgers University Computer Center, who suggested ways and means to code and analyze the mass of questionnaire responses. I am grateful to my neighbor Mary O'Donnell, of Tunbridge, Vermont, for starting the typing of the manuscript and to Kathleen Jones, who works near me in University College, for finishing the job in first-class fashion.

MATTHEW RADOM

New Brunswick, New Jersey
April, 1970

THE SOCIAL SCIENTIST IN AMERICAN INDUSTRY

INTRODUCTION

1

This is a book about a new type of scientist, the social scientist who is employed full-time in American industry. He has become an important part of that group of professionals who bring specialized knowledge, talent, and experience to the decision-making process. John Galbraith, who used the term "technostructure" to describe this group, went so far as to say that this group of specialists—not the general management—is the guiding intelligence, the brain, of the enterprise today.[1] His assertion will no doubt be frowned upon by general managers. The fact is, however, that distinctions between line and staff management are becoming blurred.

Harrington Emerson saw in the German general staff over fifty years ago the power of specialists in an organization. Emerson wrote that the Prussian army in the decade 1860–70 became what it was not because of men and arms but because of Von Moltke's creation of the general staff, whose combined wisdom was the means to arrive at sound decisions that accomplished pre-planned objectives.[2]

It has been stated by a number of experts concerned with America's manpower resources that the long-range objectives of the United States may become limited or may not be realized because of shortages in the number and quality of its highly trained manpower. Serious social and economic problems are besetting the country, the impact of which is being felt by all sectors of the economy. Leland Haworth, in his testimony before a committee of the Senate, strongly confirmed the need for the establishment of a national foundation for social sciences and said, "I think that the solution of many of the most crucial problems that the country faces, in fact, the world faces, are going to depend very, very substantially on the social sciences and on their integration with the natural sciences and engineering."[3] Yet, in recent years, major concern has been expressed over the shortage of physical scientists and engineers, even though scientists and educators have long warned against the dangers of letting advances in the natural sciences outrun those of the social sciences.

Employers in all sectors of the economy, especially those in private industry, have made extraordinary efforts to induce highly trained physical scientists, mathematicians, and engineers to work in their organizations. Resentment has been stirred up in other countries by the so-called "brain drain" of their own university-trained products by higher-salaried job offers of American employers. Some of the top managers in larger companies, however, have realized that the complex problems they are being called upon to solve have produced a need to have other highly trained people close to the centers of decision making, people trained in economics, psychology, sociology, statistics, and other social sciences.

This book will examine the role of social scientists in industry, why they chose private enterprise in which to actualize their professional training, how they feel about their careers in this sector of the economy, and why some—not very many—leave industry.

A second purpose of the research was to determine whether the research findings from studies of physical scientists in industry can be applied to social scientists in similar settings. To accomplish this aspect, the same questions asked of industrial scientists and engineers with Ph.D. degrees by Donald Pelz and

Frank Andrews were used in the questionnaires administered to the research population in this study.⁴ As we shall see, there are many comparable findings from both groups but, in many important respects, the respondents in the two groups differ in their perceptions of role, motivation, and career outlook as professionals. These differences are very important for better understanding of how such highly trained individuals can optimize their contributions to our economy.

Orth, Bailey, and Wolek asserted in their book on administering research and development people that the existing beliefs, theories, and practices of management generally prevalent today "will disclose a well-nigh total inapplicability to the management of R & D departments. It is an inadequacy nearly at its bankrupt worst in dealing with professional personnel."⁵ If such statements have validity and can be applied generally, then such serious indictments should be documented insofar as social scientists in industry are concerned. The research undertaken for this book was in part motivated by a restiveness to accept such sweeping generalizations. Direct contact with social scientists in industry did not fully support such assertions.

A third purpose of this book is to record the references to relevant literature that were located after a thorough search of ten years' of publication of *The American Behavioral Scientist, Dissertation Abstracts,* and *Psychological Abstracts* as well as references to social scientists in industry in the professional journals of the economics, psychology, sociology, and statistics associations. These searches produced surprisingly little on the subject under discussion here. Considerable research has been done on physical scientists in industry, and reference will be made to some of these books and articles reporting the findings, particularly to test some of the all-encompassing statements made about professionals in industry.

SOME DEFINITIONS

Some of the employment data reported in various studies of scientists under the heading "industry" were found confusing. Organizations such as Rand Corporation, Mitre Corporation, Systems Development Corporation, and others of the type that devote all or virtually all of their efforts to serving agencies of the United States government should be separated from purely private enterprises when comparisons are made of the type that will be undertaken here. Some of the professional associations list self-employed under "industry." The American Economic Association used the catchall category of "business" for every type of non-academic or non-governmental activity, including labor unions. The National Science Foundation in assembling data for the National Register of Scientific and Technical Personnel makes a clear-cut distinction in employment categories of respondents, and lists "private industry or business" separately. In this book, all references to "industry" will be based on the NSF definition.

A more difficult problem arose in defining "scientist." Is a person a scientist if he holds the terminal degree in his field, or is he anyone working professionally in that field? Eligibility criteria for inclusion in the National Register is delegated to the cooperating professional societies. There are wide differences in the criteria. For example, the American Chemical Society considers a person to be a qualified chemist if he is employed in a position requiring a bachelor's degree in chemistry and working in a position using knowledge from that branch of science. The Federation of American Societies for Experimental Biology, on the other hand, includes in its membership only those who hold the doctorate in experimental biology and have had several years of research experience in that field.

Dael Wolfle was confronted with a similar problem of definition when he reported on the supply of scientific manpower at a National Science Foundation meeting in 1952. In his paper, he outlined the problem and his solution:

If scientists were as easy to identify as policemen or Army officers, we could go about the country, count them, and have a fairly definitive figure for the number of scientists in the country. But they are not, and no one can state a meaningful figure for the number of scientists until he has first explained how liberally he defines a scientist. My own definition—for this paper—is simple. It includes all whom the American Chemical Society would consider chemists, whether they belong to the ACS or not, all whom the American Institute of Physics would call physicists, etc. That is not a rigorous definition of a scientist, but it indicates the nature of the group to be considered. It includes the much larger number of people working at the journeyman professional level in the sciences as well as eminent research scholars and other scientific leaders.[6]

In searching for a rigorous definition of "industrial social scientist," it was decided to include only those with doctorates in their field and employed full-time in private industry. The assumption was made that when a person undertakes long-term professional training for a scientific field, he is very likely to be found working in that field. Ewan Clague and Morton Levine asserted that virtually all Ph.D.s in economics enter the profession, whereas only a fraction of those with lower degrees in the same field work as economists.[7]

Finally, we must define "social scientist." The most commonly accepted definition is that one who was trained professionally in anthropology, economics, history, linguistics, political science, psychology, sociology, and statistics could be designated as a social scientist.

THE RESEARCH POPULATION

A total of 462 social scientists working full-time in industry and randomly selected from the membership lists of the professional societies was contacted.* The cooperation was excellent:

---

* Practically all of the sociologists working in industry were contacted, because the total was small.

of those asked for interviews, two-thirds agreed. Almost sixty per cent of the questionnaires were completed and returned to the writer.

When the questionnaires and interview notes were compiled, a total of 231 cases were finally used distributed as follows:

Economists	90	Sociologists	22
Psychologists	95	Statisticians	24

The most recent report of the number of Ph.D. social scientists in industry, compiled by the National Science Foundation, shows a total of 1658 in the fields indicated:

Psychology	1001	Sociology	35
Economics	405	Linguistics	20
Statistics	151	Anthropology	10
Political Science	36		

The 1968 National Register data were based on usable returns from 297,942 completed questionnaires. These data represented about 60 per cent of all scientists who were asked to supply information to the National Science Foundation. The statistics for those holding the Ph.D. in their fields showed that 111,206 were doctorate holders. Of this Ph.D. total, 30,378, or a little over a quarter, were social scientists. A further breakdown into employment categories revealed that 1658, or a little over 5 per cent of all Ph.D. social scientists in the National Register were employed full-time in industry.[8]

The 231 cases in this study represent a little over 11 per cent of the social scientists in industry in the National Register. They were located in 22 states and the District of Columbia working in 95 different companies. Half of the companies were in manufacturing. The remainder were about equally divided between finance (banking, insurance, investment houses), service (advertising, communications, management consulting, and opinion research), public utilities and transportation, and research laboratories.

From the tables below, it will be seen that the social scientists in this study are in the prime of life. They hold responsible positions in staff management in their companies. With the exception of statisticians, two-thirds or more were in top or middle management and not fewer than half were receiving $20,000 or more per year in salary in 1968. It is very likely that the number in this salary bracket has increased.

Ages of Respondents in 1968

Age group	Per cent	Cumulative Per cent
under 33	1	
33 to 37	5	6
38 to 42	24	30
43 to 47	29	59
48 to 52	24	83
53 to 57	10	93
58 to 62	6	99
63 or over	1	100

Position level in an organization is the most commonly accepted criterion of importance in the management hierarchy. Classification as to position levels was determined as follows:

Top Management: Has the title of president, vice-president, treasurer, comptroller, or comparable top level positions and reports directly to the chairman of the board or the president.

Middle Management: Has the title of director of research, director of personnel, or department head of a staff function, and reports to a vice-president.

Bottom Management: Is a supervisor, group leader, or other first- or second-level management position and reports to a middle management official of the company. This group also includes those who are specialists or members of technical staffs.

Position Level and Field of Social Science

	Per cent			
	Top	Middle	Bottom	Total
Economists	33	37	30	100
Psychologists	21	43	36	100
Sociologists	40	30	30	100
Statisticians	4	26	70	100

Present Age and Position in the Organization

	Per cent		
Present Age (1968)	Top Management	Middle Management	Bottom Management
Under 33	0	0	1
33 to 37	0	1	15
38 to 42	17	16	35
43 to 47	29	33	23
48 to 52	29	33	15
53 to 57	12	15	5
58 to 62	12	1	6
63 and over	1	1	0
	100	100	100
42 or under	17	17	51
43 or over	83	83	49

An analysis of the above shows that the most important factor related to level in the organization is age. However, in the case of statisticians, it is apparent that professionals in this field of social science have not yet emerged as prominently into the higher levels of staff management as have their colleagues in the other sciences. In later chapters, when we shall be examining data both from respondents and from other sources, there will be further exploration of the relationships among field of science, age, and position in the organization.

There is another piece of information that is relevant to our understanding of factors bearing on position level and that is the relationship between age on attaining the doctorate and its effect, if any, on present level in the management. The table below gives these data.

Even if we allow for the biasing effect of the position levels of statisticians, it is apparent that there is a slight advantage for advancement in the hierarchy, for those contemplating a career in industry, in going on to the doctorate on completeion of undergraduate studies.

To complete the background information, we should know something about the effect on position in the management of

Age on Attaining Doctorate and Present Managerial Level

	Per cent		
Age at Ph.D.	*Top Management*	*Middle Management*	*Bottom Management*
25 or under	7	7	14
26 to 28	12	21	29
29 to 31	38	28	29
32 to 34	19	24	21
35 to 39	21	16	5
40 to 44	3	0	2
45 and over	0	4	0
	100	100	100
Up to 31	57	56	72
32 or over	43	44	28

the type of experience the respondents had before joining their
present organizations:

**Type of Work Experience with Ph.D. Before Joining Present Organization
and Level in Management**

	Per cent			
Came from	*Top Management*	*Middle Management*	*Bottom Management*	*Total*
Another company	29	38	33	100
College or univ.	26	46	28	100
Government	40	25	35	100
Non-profit org.	22	44	34	100
Completion of Ph.D. studies	15	34	51	100

If we consider those in middle management together with the
respondents in top management as important members of the
technostructure, then we must conclude that some kind of experience after attainment of the Ph.D. has significant advantage
for moving into higher levels of management. This conclusion
is supported by salary data, a readily recognizable criterion of
"success" in our society. The next two tables will reveal some
interesting data on this aspect of the picture. The interviews

and questionnaires were completed in 1968; it is likely that the amounts shown have since increased.

Present Salary and Field of Social Science

	Per cent			
	$10,000 to $15,000	*$15,000 to $20,000*	*Over $20,000*	*Total*
Economists	5	25	70	100
Psychologists	20	24	56	100
Sociologists	5	20	75	100
Statisticians	12	38	50	100

Came from Work Experience with Ph.D. and Present Salary

	Per cent			
Industry	9	28	63	100
College or univ.	7	28	65	100
Government	8	25	67	100
Non-profit org.	7	29	64	100
No experience	25	25	50	100

We can now summarize our findings about the typical social scientist in industry. He is now in his early forties, has an important position in management, and is well paid. He came to his present organization with professional experience in another company, government, or non-profit organization or was a college or university teacher at that time. He is working at the corporate headquarters of his company unless he is in the field of statistics. Statisticians in industry, holding the doctorate, are mainly to be found in research laboratories of commercial companies.

SOME QUESTIONS TO BE ANSWERED

The basic purpose of this study is to determine from the data to be presented in later chapters the answers to a number of questions that should be raised about social scientists in industry. From the answers, it is hoped that we can have a good understanding of how industrial social scientists see their world of work, what the sources of satisfaction and dissatisfaction are, and what their career plans are. In addition, we shall be testing certain assertions, assumptions, or findings in other studies of professionals in industry, mainly physical scientists, to determine whether the respondents in this study should be seen in the same way by their employers. The questions follow:

1. How and when did social scientists decide on their future careers? Did those now in industry have such careers in mind early in their collegiate years?

2. Do social scientists seek positions in industry primarily because of higher salaries than can be expected in government, universities, or non-profit organizations?

3. Do social scientists in industry have any desire to move into position of line responsibility in their companies and away from professional careers in their fields of science?

4. The majority of social scientists employed in industry are to be found in large companies. It has been asserted by several writers that large corporations stifle individuality and creativity. Do social scientists in industry feel stifled and less creative than their colleagues outside of industry?

5. Do social scientists have the same or different feelings about their work, their colleagues, and their organizational superiors as do physical scientists in similar settings?

6. A number of writers have stated that physical scientists in industry are more concerned about how they appear in the eyes of their fellow scientists in the profession than they are about their standing in the company. Simon Marcson coined the phrase "colleague authority" to describe this feeling.[9] Do social scientists exhibit similar attitudes toward colleague authority as do their physical science counterparts in industry?

7. Do social scientists move about or do they settle down into careers in a particular company? If they have desires to leave their present positions, what are the motivations for such feelings?

8. Why do some social scientists leave industry? Would they

be willing to accept another industrial position? If so, under what conditions or circumstances?

9. How do social scientists react to the accusation made by Loren Baritz that they are merely paid servants of industrial management and willing to do its bidding even to the extent of distorting research findings in order to satisfy the desires of their employers?[10]

These are some of the major questions we shall try to answer in the chapters that follow. There may be others, no doubt, in the reader's mind. Perhaps the data to be examined and analyzed will provide some clues to possible answers for such questions as well as open up some thinking for additional research in the same general area.

We shall begin by examining the role of the social scientist in industry. What does he do within a private company? Each field of social science will be taken up separately.

THE ROLE OF THE SOCIAL
SCIENTIST IN INDUSTRY

2

Most of what we know about the roles of social scientists in various settings has been described by the practitioners in a few articles or in chapters of books that have appeared rather recently.[1] The latest survey of the work of social scientists in industry was undertaken by Simon Marcson in 1963. He found that, characteristically, social scientists are not utilized in industry with the same specificity as in a university;[2] social scientists are often found working in research activities that sometimes seem unrelated to the field of their advanced degrees. However, in the larger organizations, it was found that there were discrete roles as will be seen when we read the responses of those interviewed.

First, let us take a look at some of the descriptions that were found in the literature. They will be presented under headings of the various social sciences commonly found in industry.

Economists

At a symposium held at the Harvard Graduate School of Business in 1943 a number of practitioners from industry met to discuss the work of economists in corporate enterprises. Paul

Weber of Hercules Powder Company dated economic research in his company from 1934 onward. Charles Young of Westinghouse gave 1937 as the year when the office of economist was established in his company.[3]

Clark Teitsworth conducted a survey of five hundred "blue chip" companies in 1950 to find out how many employed full-time economists. He estimated that about a third of the companies had such specialists on their staffs. Teitsworth also tried to summarize the duties of the industrial economists but he found such variation that he selected one reply as the most representative description of the role of the company economist:[4]

He keeps management informed of general business trends and developments in this country and abroad. He is particularly useful in providing lessons from history since he can take a long look back and can see the most recent developments in perspective. His greatest contribution can probably be made in the area of business expansion.

Roy Reirson, a senior vice-president and chief economist for one of the world's largest banks, reported to an international conference of commercial bank economists the results of a questionnaire he sent to thirty bank officers in the United States who were known or presumed to be engaged in economic work for their organizations. Reirson summarized the responses as follows:

Overwhelmingly, the economists' duties are concerned primarily with research and analysis of general economic conditions. About a third of the respondents stated that they were involved with analyses of specific industries. . . . It deserves to be noted that in almost all instances where general economic research is not described as a primary responsibility, it seems to be because the economist is heavily engaged in portfolio administration. Every respondent, regardless of his specific duties, emphasizes that his work is designed to support the management and the operations of his institution. Forecasts are prepared by a large majority of the bank economists on business conditions and commodity prices. Surprisingly, credit demand and money supply are less frequently the objects of the bank economists' forecasting endeavors, and the demand-supply situation in the investment markets ranks last.[5]

At a National Science Foundation meeting in 1958, Robert Johnson, Western Electric Company's economist, described a new role for his colleagues in industry—especially in manufacturing operations—of "logistics research." He defined this approach as a means of recognizing a problem needing solution, analyzing the problem to understand its parameters, developing a hypothesis for obtaining a solution, and testing that hypothesis. "Frequently in logistics research," he said, "the hypothesis can be mathematically formulated. This permits evaluations on paper before a solution involving men, money, and materials is committed." Johnson went on to say that his work involved problems connected with distribution of products, plant location, product mix, inventory, and process scheduling.[6]

During the interviews with social scientists in industry, questions were asked to find out if their organizations had job descriptions covering their duties and responsibilities. The general consensus was that it would be very difficult to write such descriptions, as the job depended almost entirely on the person who filled it. The president of Columbia Broadcasting System, Dr. Frank Stanton, was quoted by a *Business Week* writer as saying that he could not write a job description for the company's chief economist but the magazine writer's perception of the role is interesting for our understanding:

No one person at Columbia Broadcasting System knows what David M. Blank does with all his time. The 43 year old Ph.D. heads a small office for economic analysis that services CBS's operating divisions and staff executives. Blank, like most business economists, is the man in charge of his company's forecasting operations. But, unlike many of his colleagues, he spends less time on forecasts than on economic analyses in the broad spectrum of the company's operations. When Blank isn't busy erasing doubts, he's often busy creating them. "One thing our group has done," he says rather proudly, "is to let people around here know when we see something important." Blank's quasi-academic operation is a reflection partly of his own fondness for research and partly of Stanton's, a Ph.D. in psychology, who once headed CBS' central research group.[7]

WHAT THE RESPONDENTS SAID
ABOUT THEIR ROLES

An economist in a chemical company:

I majored in market research for my Ph.D. and that has been one of my main functions here. Our group gets its assignments from all divisions of the company; how we do them is up to us. As I'm the only economist in the company, one of my responsibilities is to keep the company advised on what's going on in business generally and how these developments may affect our company's business. People have aproached me to help on day-to-day problems in connection with planning that I get involved with.

The manager of the planning department of an international oil company:

Our company is interested in the potential for our products in under-developed countries. I go into these countries to see what methods our marketing people in the United States use that may be applicable to the country being studied. I make forecasts of that country's energy requirements, look at the growth and capability for increases in GNP by estimating from population increases and other factors what the highway needs are going to be, the number of trucks and cars that one day may be using those highways, and the like. In the United States, our group makes studies of newly planned interstate highway systems not yet constructed. How will they affect our company's business? The problem of land values arises—what investments can be made now that will increase in value as the system goes into operation? I give advice and counsel, when it's asked for, on all projects being planned.

The vice-president of an opinion research organization said that when he first joined the company he was given a specific assignment—to design a market research plan. After that project was completed, he was asked to help on a number of different kinds of problems for the company's clients. "I usually pick the ones that appeal to me the most," he said. "The client decides what he wants and I develop the means of getting the necessary information for analysis. I'm limited, of course, by the size of the budget."

The director of research for a large advertising agency said he didn't see much connection between his training as an economist and his present duties. "I see myself primarily as a manager of research people to see that the needed research gets done. Our kind of work involves working with behavioral scientists. Frankly, I have a hard time understanding them."

The director of corporate research in a manufacturing company:

My title really best describes what I do. I started here in the Planning Department but over a period of time, economic research became more and more important. I have built a department of twenty people and we get into all kinds of corporate problems.

Psychologists

Of the four fields of social science usually found being utilized by industry, psychology may well be called "the senior science." As far back as 1914, tests were being developed and used for the selection of telephone operators, telegraphists, and streetcar motormen. According to Morris Viteles, early experiments in the application of psychology to industry were limited to the development of selection techniques.[8] Later, especially after World War I—when industrial psychologists took their army experience back with them into civilian life—work began on research in training, accident reduction, fatigue, analysis of work methods, and other areas involving work and workers.

The space age has propelled psychologists into new areas of investigation. Some of the problems of man in space are being studied by human-factors experts (sometimes known as "engineering psychologists") in the aerospace industry. The last decade has shown an interesting development in this field where the orientation is not so much to fit the man to the machine—as in the past—but rather to fit the machine to the man.[9]

Psychologists are also involved in the burgeoning field of data processing and systems analysis. At I.B.M., where a good many professional social scientists are employed, the general area is called "Systems Engineering." Systems engineering, in relation to data processing, means solving problems with computers.[10]

Morton Feinberg and Jacob Lefkowitz sampled executive opinion of the work of psychologists in industry.[11] Asked if they would hire an industrial psychologist if they had the authority to do so, two-thirds said that they would. Those who favored adding such a professional to the staff were then asked to designate the areas in which they thought industrial psychologists should work. The replies were as folows:

Should work in	Per cent
Employee motivation, morale	61
Employee training, selection, and promotion	54
Executive selection, training, and promotion	51
Human factors engineering	27
Consumer research	10
Production efficiency, accident prevention	3

It is of some interest that the last two items mentioned received so few check marks by the executives. It is likely that they still feel that salesmen are the best judges of consumer preferences, and that industrial engineers should be responsible for production efficiency and plant safety, despite evidence that shows the need for social science research in these areas.

In a poll taken by the Education and Training Committee of the division of industrial psychology of the American Psychological Association a few years ago, psychologists employed in industry indicated the areas of most needed post-doctoral training as follows:[12]

Computer methods	Labor-management relations
Group behavior	Motivation
Group dynamics	Opinion attitudes and morale
Group incentives	Organization planning
Group performance	Organization theory
Information systems	Probability theory
Linear and non-linear programing	Statistical decision theory

It is clear from the listed areas that industrial psychologists are being drawn into problems that were not stressed in their earlier training, or they foresee the possibility of getting involved in such problems, or both.

ROLE PERCEPTION BY THOSE INTERVIEWED

Psychologist on the technical staff of a communications company research laboratory:

When I first came here I was encouraged to look around and see what I would like to work on. My special field is speech and I saw very quickly that research in speech perception should provide not only interesting work for me but should also pay off for the company. Self-initiation is okay if you have ideas but after a while you have to get ideas from colleagues in other fields in the lab. I found that my work got me more and more involved in problems of information retrieval and circuitry and away from clinical approaches. I could have continued speech pathology but practical application to communications systems interested me much more.

Director of research at a large advertising agency:

When people at decision-making levels in our client companies need research for trying to understand customer research, they come to us for help. They expect me to decide what methods to use and what kind of data to collect to help solve the problem. All research designs have to have my approval. The top managements are usually very good about giving me plenty of budget flexibility. My work has gotten me involved with marketing and public opinion research so I find that I am less interested in the annual meetings of the

American Psychological Association, and spending more time listening to what goes on at the American Marketing Association and the American Public Opinion Research Association. A third of my time is spent on administration—which I don't particularly like—but I have learned to handle it along with my main activities.

The head of manpower planning at the corporate office of a major oil company said that his primary job was to develop manpower information systems based on the personnel records that are sent in from the operating companies. As company needs arise to fill managerial, professional, and technical positions throughout the corporation, possible candidates are obtained from the company's manpower information system. In addition, individual training programs are developed for such people, especially those who are moved into or out of overseas operations. In recent years, he has been called on to help with executive appraisals and believes he will have to develop a company-wide appraisal system to provide objective information that can be relied upon when executive posts are to be filled. His unit did not exist before he came to the company.

Management development advisor in a large manufacturing company:

Before I came here, the company had no well-designed program for the development of present and future management. The company was faced with an unusual number of high level replacements at that time and so before I could really design a long-range program, I was asked to use my training as a clinical psychologist to advise on filling vacancies from within the company or interviewing new hires. For the first two years I worked alone and had many, many conferences with heads of the operating units. After we met the most pressing problems, I was encouraged by top management to build a research group and start working on a long-range approach. I now have three Ph.D.s helping me in management development and another is spending full time on methodology. We maintain a central service for all branches and functions of the company and are constantly called upon to help with recruitment, selection, training, and development—particularly of management personnel from the foremen on up to top management.

The director of research at a major broadcasting company said that he had been a consultant when he had been a college teacher and in one study he was asked to advise on how people receive information and what media had the biggest effect. "I was very much impressed by the effect television had on people," he said, "and I was asked to continue the research as a full-time job here. I started pretty much as a one-man shop but now we have our own department that has done all of the research on all media. My primary job now is to plan research and see that it gets done."

Vice-president in an opinion-survey company:

The company hired me because they knew that I had done some work for the government in motivation research—I guess you'd call it propaganda research. Methodological development is crucial in measuring attitudes; that's my special field of interest, working on methodology. If an inquiry comes in from a client company, we look it over to see if our methods can help. If the project looks like it should be handled by a psychologist, I'm asked to take it on in my group. Sometimes I work with other social scientists on their projects.

Sociologists

The first large-scale sociological research in industry was carried out by Elton Mayo and his associates from Harvard at the Hawthorne Works of the Western Electric Company in the early 1930's. It is generally conceded by sociologists that the failure of the Western Electric illumination experiments intrigued the top management so much that it was determined to continue its search for the causes of motivation of employees, thus bringing about the birth of industrial sociology in America.

John Riley, a long-time teacher of sociology at Rutgers University and now a vice-president at one of the world's largest insurance companies, pointed out that not more than a generation ago professors of sociology were to be found only in academia. The situation is changing, he believes, because many types of organizations need some systematic knowledge of human behavior. He cited his own experience of being called upon by industry:

> After nearly thirty years as a teacher, I joined a large insurance company, with the unprecedented mission of forging a basic research link between that large and complex world of affairs, on the one hand, and the world of sociological ideas and scholarship on the other. My immediate task is to illuminate some of the ways in which behavioral science knowledge and techniques are being applied in contemporary American society.[13]

Robert Carlson, a sociologist in a large corporation, sees the work of industrial sociologists as falling into two broad areas: (1) the influence of the work group on productivity, morale, internal communication, and related topics and (2) the size and composition of audiences for the messages put out by industrial corporations. [14]

Leo Bogart, vice-president and director of research for a publishers' association, believes that sociologists have only lately realized that market research is a field for which their training especially fits them. He points out that vast sums are expended to study the attitudes, preferences, and choices of consumers, and that these studies are being increasingly relied upon by business managements in their decision-making. Bogart, in another article, underlined the important role of sociologists in public opinion research. He feels that these social scientists, as well as others, have made many valuable contributions on problems involving relations with the public, and have often revealed incongruities between managements' intuitive views of particular situations and the actual evidence that was developed by sociological research.[15]

Simon Marcson found in his survey of social science in industry that sociologists often worked in activities quite similar to those engaged in by industrial psychologists. For example, in research projects involving employees, markets, organization planning, and communications within companies and with their publics, sociologists or psychologists were both heavily involved.[16]

SELF-PERCEPTION OF ROLE BY SOCIOLOGISTS IN INDUSTRY

Advisor in the public relations department of an international oil company:

When I first came to this company, I had the typical academician's attitude toward private enterprise, that a commercial organization didn't really want sociological research—it wanted to use me for creating favorable propaganda for the company. I soon found out, however, that top management had considerable interest in finding out what sort of image it had with the public, its customers, and its shareholders as well as employees. It happens that I have a deep interest in developments in the Middle East and, since the company had large investments in that area, there was agreement that I should undertake a research study of communication links in that part of the world. My research, not surprisingly, revealed that company officials had been thinking of ways to communicate with the nationals in pre-conceived terms of reference that just didn't hold in the region.

On other projects, I found that I had to take a much broader look at the various problems in order to make myself effective as a trained sociologist. This didn't mean that I abandoned the research approach; not at all. It did mean that I had to lose some of my academic notions of how to work in the real world.

A sociologist who is a member of the technical staff at the research laboratory of a large communications company said that his particular interest is trying to find out why people organize themselves in the ways that they do, and how bureaucracies are formed. "I've been working on these interests here," he said. "The company has given me a completely free hand to

pick the projects I want to work on but my professional colleagues keep asking me to help them with their projects. At this
point I don't know if I'm an industrial sociologist or an industrial psychologist."

Vice-president and director of social research at an insurance
company:

The company brought me in because it thought I could help it to
understand where it was now, where it was going, and why, in the
next fifty or so years in a social environment that the president of
the company thought would be vastly different from today. I feel a
little like a missionary, coming out of the academic world, but I am
confident that I can do some important work here. I have made a
number of presentations to the Board of Directors, all men in high
positions in their own organizations, and I feel from the questions
and comments that they have learned something from my work. Of
course, I have learned plenty, too.

The company looks to me to select areas of worth-while research.
I don't actually do the research; we farm it out to universities and
research centers. Obviously, I have the responsibility to see to it that
the research meets rigid standards and then I translate the results
for those who need to understand the outcomes for their own guidance. It seems to me that I am more academic-minded now than
when I was at a university where I had to worry about staff, teaching schedules, and tender loving care of the younger faculty members.

Vice-president and director of research for a consulting company:

Although my doctorate was in Sociology, it seems to me that my
work is really in Psychology. I have always been interested in research and this job gives me an opportunity to do such work here
on a large scale. I developed a perception laboratory here and,
when the word got around that we did this kind of experimentation,
a lot of contracts came to the company although that was not the
reason I developed the lab. I'm interested in the meanings of social
forces and so is the company, so I guess we've made a good match.

The director of research at a large advertising agency felt that he was not really a scientist in the full sense of that word. "A scientist is concerned with the development of a coherent body of theory," he explained, "but our work is designed to solve marketing problems. Our efforts are devoted to the rational development and criticism of advertising strategies and tactics in particular and of marketing strategies and tactics in general."

Statisticians

Although the American Statistical Association, founded in 1839, is the oldest professional society of social scientists, statisticians are the newest to be employed full-time in American industry in research and other activities. Statistics has been a major tool in all of the sciences for a good many years. In the past decade, however, statisticians have moved into areas far removed from the original impetus of collecting vital statistics for others. James Newman has pointed out that the field of statistics now offers a major new development known as statistical decision theory. "Departing from tradition," he wrote, "this approach shows how both judgment and statistical evidence should be combined in the making of decisions."[17]

Theodore Brown saw the need for mathematical and statistical techniques for decision-making in business over thirty years ago. He observed that a better understanding of business problems required the adoption of such techniques to produce appropriate solutions. "Although application of mathematical and statistical techniques for the solution of engineering problems has long been accepted as indispensable," he wrote, "their use in administrative problems at present is increasing."[18]

Walter Hoadley, a former president of the American Statistical Association, feels that industry statisticians have made their greatest contribution to policy formulation and the decision process. In his presidential address to the A.S.A. in 1959 he said:

Policy decisions invariably concern the future. Hence, if statistics and statistical techniques are to be useful, they too must point to the future. In my judgment, statisticians should have a continuing and aggressive interest in data interpretation and in forecasting as an aid to policy-making in whatever capacity and field they serve since presumably they know more about Statistics than anyone else. In every field in which we are working, data interpretation for forecasting and decision-making are unavoidable and inseparable.

Hoadley went on to say that many top-level executives have complained that statisticians will do an enormous amount of work but stop short of making a positive contribution to policy. "That contribution," he pointed out, "should be a helpful interpretation of the data, a suggestion, or a recommendation for future action based on the statistician's findings."[19]

William Butler, vice-president and head of his organization's economic and statistical research group, refined the role of the statistician in business organizations under four headings:[20]

1. Identifying the problems that are important for the business and are susceptible of statistical analysis;
2. Developing an organization that can assemble and analyze the vast mass of sophisticated data that management needs to have interpreted;
3. Working out effective methods of communication to provide a translation of the results of the technical analyses into language that can be readily understood by non-technicians; and
4. Setting up the channels of communication to transmit the results of statistical and economic research to management.

SELF-PERCEPTION OF STATISTICIANS OF THEIR ROLES IN INDUSTRY

Member of the technical staff at a research laboratory of a communications company:

In mathematical statistics, a good problem is a valuable thing; it's something that people in our field almost covet. There is a question of beauty involved, elegance—if you know what I mean. Here at the lab, we're not that concerned with the beauty of a particular problem but we try to find such problems. Research in this field is not doing something that someone tells you to do; it's finding out what needs to be done. Everyone would like to be free as a bird but on the other hand, he would like to see something done with his work, not just do it for amusement. Other people should want to use your work. That is why, when we have vacancies in our group, we try to fill them with people who are not only good statisticians but who are also people with wide interests. I find that by getting out and meeting people in other departments, there are all kinds of problems to work on. Of course, I try to pick the ones that have beauty.

A statistician in the actuarial department of a large insurance company said, "there are very few Ph.D.s in statistics doing my kind of work. We are developing a research program here that involves building statistical and mathematical models. It's hard to see right now how my work will be used here but I haven't been with this company very long—less than a year. It's my first job since acquiring the doctorate."

Member of the technical staff of a research laboratory of a manufacturing company:

I first went to work for a large glass manufacturing company when I received my doctorate in statistics. I was the only statistician with that level of training in the company. I felt very frustrated by the feeling that I was really working in the field of applied mechanics which was not at all what I wanted. Since coming here, I've become involved in all kinds of interesting problems such as marketing, economic analysis, manpower planning, and even product improvement.

Many people in my field feel a little self-conscious if they're not working on product improvement but I don't have that feeling at all. I know the corporation has to make a profit but I also feel it's our job to do basic research. There are too many examples of how basic research helped the company to develop new products so I don't worry about it.

The majority of respondents whose doctorate was in statistics were located in research laboratories, usually for companies located far enough away from the eastern seaboard so that per-

sonal interview was not practicable. The written responses to
the questionnaire were quite varied but, in general, the descriptions above are representative of the replies. There is hardly
any area in which the impact of statistics has been felt more
strongly than in business.

Summary

As was stated in the beginning of this chapter, social scientists
are often found working in research and other activities that
seem unrelated to the fields in which they received their doctoral training. As will be seen in later chapters, some welcome
moving into new areas, but others tend to restrict themselves to
their particular fields. It was of some significance that directors
of research often were in charge of all social science research
being done in or for the company, and that no particular branch
of science seemed to be selected for administration of this work.
It may be useful for the reader, however, in summarizing the
roles of the different sciences, to do so under separate headings.

Economists

Much depends on the type of organization when considering
the role of the professional economist in private enterprise. In
financial institutions such as banks, insurance companies, and
investment houses, and in manufacturing companies economists
are much more involved with long-range planning than is the
case in advertising, public relations, or consulting organizations. It is significant that no economists were found in research
laboratories. This probably reflects industry's opinion that basic
research in economics should be left to the academicians.

Although professional economists are usually found in staff
management as advisors to the line, a fair number have moved
into decision-making posts at high levels. Among the respondents in this study, all of the presidents, executive vice-presidents,
treasurers and other officers of companies were economists. This
finding can best be explained by the fact that economists are

working with and analyzing data which affect the very life of the organizations in which they work. The fact that top managers seek the advice of their economists before making decisions of a long-range nature, usually involving large capital investments, puts the economist in a particularly strategic position when top posts are to be filled.

Industrial executives, recognizing the close relationship between well-planned and executed research and development expenditures and the growth of their companies, have come to realize the long-run implications of vigorous research programs. This realization was demonstrated during the 1957–58 recession when capital expenditures for plant and equipment experienced a decline while expenditures for research and development increased.[21] Several of the economists in this study thought that they played a vital role in the determination of how much of the company's resources, both financial and manpower, should be allocated to research.

Economists in business have usually been identified with forecasting economic trends. The economists in this study almost always mentioned this aspect of their work as being of greatest importance to their managements. At the same time, they were willing to admit that much needs to be done to improve forecasting, especially through research in a particular organization. They pointed out that in its simplest and least dependable form, economic forecasting simply involves a guess by a businessman as to future conditions, often based on hunch or intuition. With a professional economist available to him, much closer attention can be paid by a top executive to economic data and their analysis, and professional standards will not allow the economist to deviate from fact to fancy. In his role, he must be guided by his professional training and his ability to select significant from insignificant data for analysis to guide the decison makers.

Psychologists

In the history of industrial psychology, the use of psychological tests for selection, placement, and guidance has been the foremost activity of professionals employed by managements to help with these kinds of personnel problems. There is no reason to believe that testing will become any less important but the scope of the industrial psychologist's role in industry has expanded into many more areas of organizational life. In a booklet of the American Psychological Association's division of industrial psychology, the appendix lists 158 different kinds of problems in which industrial psychologists are currently involved and in which practical research has been conducted.[22]

In a fairly recent book on industrial psychology, the author succinctly described the present-day activities of professionals in this field:

> The psychologist in industry does far more than give tests, a job popularly believed to be his activity. True, he has designed the tests and validated them to see if they accurately predict what they are supposed to. But in the main the psychologist in industry has turned the testing program over to others. He is now advising the industrial relations department on the company's pending contract negotiations with the union, or he is designing a study to determine the buying habits of a suburban housewife as she walks through the local supermarket. In one hour, the industrial psychologist may be discussing the psychology of learning with the company's training director; in the next hour, he may be participating in a conference on a morale survey to be conducted in an out-of-town plant. . . . He helps to improve safety programs, and he works with the engineers on human aspects of equipment design. He may draw up a plan for executive development of newly-hired college graduates on one day and discuss the problems of aging employees the next. From personnel selection to training, from supervision to job evaluation, from career planning to labor relations, the industrial psychologist moves in a wide and every-varying scene.[23]

With the rapid increase in technology and the concomitant human problems, top executives have come to realize that considerable attention must be paid to the stresses and strains that develop between a company's goal of efficient operations and the employee's desire to retain his individuality in a large organization. Dr. F. A. L. Holloway, president of Esso Research & Engineering Company, told the 1968 graduating class at Georgia Institute of Technology that the problem of resolving the age-old conflict between the desires of individuals to control their destinies and the need to place decisions involving many people in the hands of the "individual-group" has been with man since ancient civilization, but its recognition and resolution are becoming more and more important as society moves into large groups. He attributed much of the current protest on campuses and elsewhere to these opposing needs. In tracing the progress being made toward harmonizing individual and group goals, Dr. Hollaway said many business people are engaging applied psychologists to aid management to reappraise individual behavior and group processes. "In my own field of industrial research and engineering we are finding," he said, "that we cannot improve the innovation of material things without innovating in our organizational processes."[24]

The criteria for assessing organizational effectiveness, one of the areas that industrial psychologists are grappling with, has been at the forefront of recent social science research in corporations and other forms of activity. Thomas Mahoney wrote that the administrator or researcher seeking measures of organizational effectiveness faces a bewildering array of potentially relevant criteria. A bibliography published in 1959 lists over 370 references. "One finds relatively little consensus about actual relevance of these criteria," he stated. Most consensus appears with respect to one concept and that is goal achievement. This concept of organizational effectiveness, while valid, merely recasts the search for effectiveness criteria into a search for organizational goals."[25] There is little doubt that this complex problem, although seemingly a simple one on its face, will have to be tackled by the company itself with the aid of professional psychologists and other social scientists. There are no do-it-yourself handbooks that can do this important job.

Another area of first-rank importance, especially in the fast-developing era of high speed vehicles and the rapid communications systems accompanying them, has produced the human-factors specialist generally known as an engineering psychologist. P. M. Fitts has described engineering psychology as an activity that seeks to understand how human performance is related to task variables, especially engineering design, and to formulate theory and principles of human performance that can be applied to the design of human tasks, human-operated equipment, and man-machine systems. Fitts predicted that the work on complex computer, communication, data processing, and control systems will stimulate new types of research in engineering psychology.[26]

Joseph Engel, the president of the Operations Research Society of America, declared at a three-day forum on systems analysis and social change that as operations research experts and systems analysts move closer and closer to human beings, human life, and to its goals, they find that they are dealing progressively with more and more difficult problems. "We're very good at hardware and tactical problems and starting well-defined research and development programs. We're lousy at strategic and philosophical problems," he said. "We need to put all of our social scientists, sociologists, psychologists, all our 'people-oriented' people to work on these problems." He predicted a very long and difficult road ahead in dealing with the complex problems of modern social systems.[27] There is little doubt that industrial psychologists, including "engineering psychologists," will be called upon even more than at present to help in this ever-expanding area of social research.

We cannot conclude this part of the chapter dealing with organization roles of psychologists without some reference to a field of exploration that has only recently been given great impetus—the study of learning. As Bernard Bass and James Vaughan have pointed out, industrial psychologists are coming to the realization that in designing development programs for managers, much more attention is being paid to teaching managers how to learn. "In the past," they wrote, "an ample portion of common sense would stand a manager in good stead in this regard. However, in today's rapidly changing managerial world, common sense is not enough. To be most effective—and perhaps, eventually, even to survive as a manager, one must take cognizance of the basic principles of learning and utilize them in understanding and changing the behavior of others and oneself."[28]

Sociologists

Some of the respondents in this study felt unclear as to whether they should be seen as industrial sociologists or as industrial psychologists. There is a possibility, according to one corporation sociologist, that the industrial sociologist is sometimes perceived by his psychologist colleagues as poaching on the latters' preserves.[29] In an organization that employs both sociologists and psychologists, there may be a possibility of rivalry, or even conflict.

Sociologists in large corporations do have a special role for which their training fits them eminently, and that is in the area of understanding public opinion in a particular social setting. Industrial management has become much more sensitive to the need for understanding public attitudes. The public-be-damned era is not only over, it is an anachronism in these times. The power of the public to regulate business through government is seen as a constant threat, especially by "big business." The image or reputation of a large company is today rarely left to chance.

Alvin Gouldner has raised a basic question about the role of sociologists working in industrial organizations, and that is whether the industrial sociologist merely collects information and delivers it to the decision makers or uses the information to diagnose the problems of the organization and makes specific action recommendations. Gouldner feels that up to the present, the dominant role adopted by most sociologists has been cast in the classic utilitarian mold, that is, the policy maker defines his difficulties as deriving from inadequate knowledge and calls upon the sociologist to furnish more factual data. "He operates on the assumption that, if he only had greater knowledge, his problems would capitulate," wrote Gouldner. "It is with this in mind, presumably, that he calls upon the applied sociologist. The policy-maker also tends to assume that the inadequacy of his knowledge is somehow accidental or a matter of neglect. He rarely entertains the dismaying thought that his very ignorance may be functional to him."[30] Thus, academicians like Gouldner see the role as a very limited one. It is quite evident, however, that such a limited role would not be of much interest to industrial leaders like Devereux Joseph, former chairman of the Board of the New York Life Insurance Company who asserted that large organizations like insurance companies "have to have an increasingly sophisticated knowledge of the changing behavior of human populations and also an ability to act on this knowledge to the end of bringing about a more efficient relationship between our social institutions and the larger society within which they must function."[31]

Statisticians

Statistical analysis has become a major tool of planning and control in private enterprise. Industry has found that market research, production control, budgeting, personnel research, and investment studies all require professional statisticians to either carry out the studies or work with others in analyzing data. Philip Hauser has pointed out that social science research is becoming increasingly quantitative either by means of statistical methods or direct mathematical approaches. "The application of statistical method to social phenomena and the body of propositions and theory emanating therefrom are playing a major role in the advancement of social science," he wrote.[32]

The industrial statisticians located for this study were found largely in research laboratories where they were working with both physical and social scientists in basic and applied research, as well as development. In Chapter 1 we noted that present-day statisticians in industry have not advanced as high in the management hierarchy as have their colleagues in the other social sciences. This reflects not only their late arrival on the industrial scene but also says something about the roles to which they have been assigned; their organization titles indicated that their primary function was filling helpful roles in the work of other professionals.

The industrial statistician is being called upon more and more to establish himself as an expert in experimental design, analysis of experimental data, product evaluation, and application of computers to problem solving. It is in the last-named area that the statistician has come to play a vital role in statistical theory and its application.

Statisticians specialize either in mathematical statistics or in the application of statistical methods in a particular field. A statistician who works with data on economic conditions may have the title of economist instead of statistician. On the other hand, a mathematical statistician engaged in applying probability theory to the development of new statistical methods may be classified as a mathematician.[33] Statisticians in industry tend to see themselves in the same way as the professionals they work with. As has already been stated, some do not consider themselves to be social scientists. Clarity of role of the statistician in industry awaits further development in this field.

FACTORS IN THE CAREER SELECTIONS OF SOCIAL SCIENTISTS IN INDUSTRY

3

In recent years the emphasis in the United States on the need for a college education for "success" has produced record-breaking enrollments at all institutions of higher learning. It is common experience that when one asks college-bound youngsters what they have in mind for future careers, by and large the majority have few solid ideas as to the specific kinds of occupations they intend to prepare for. In this chapter we shall not delve very far into a highly complex subject on which much has been written and little learned. However, there may be some value to young people thinking of social science careers in industry, their counselors, parents, teachers, and prospective employers in taking note of how and when the social scientists in this study determined their careers. In a later chapter we shall see that their present commitments have not veered very far from their original decisions.

RESEARCH ON OCCUPATIONAL CHOICE

There has been considerable effort expended on trying to find the determinants of occupational choice. The knowledge we have to date of the factors that influence young people as to what kind of careers to follow in adult life is sparse. In one large study, the researchers sought to develop an approach to career determination and concluded that it had been impossible to build a general theory of occupational choice from the findings of their empirical investigations. During the course of the study, Professor Donald Super of Columbia University's Teachers College was asked to review the American literature of the research in this general area. Professor Super tried to assess the findings to determine what role parents, counselors, and others played in the choice process. He concluded that there was little knowledge to be gleaned from the research findings.[1]

Robert Thorndike and Elizabeth Hagen, about ten years ago, tried to correlate later occupations of 17,000 young men who had been in the U. S. Air Force as cadets with the vast amount of data available in the official files in terms of predictive ability by factorial analysis. Little was found to support any claims that might have been made in the past about the validity of commonly used predictors:

There is no convincing evidence that aptitude tests or biographical information of the type that was available to us can predict degree of success within an occupation insofar as this is represented in the criterion measures we were able to obtain. This would suggest that we should view the long-range prediction of occupational success by aptitude tests with a great deal of skepticism and take a very restrained view as to how much can be accomplished in this direction.[2]

Eli Ginzberg believes that the decision concerning an occupational choice is, in the last analysis, a compromise whereby the individual hopes to gain the maximum degree of satisfaction out of his working life by pursuing a career in which he can make as much use as possible of his interests and capacities.[3] Douglas Bray has hypothesized that one's level of work is determined in large part by the major goals he seeks to achieve through work—such as the socio-economic status to which he aspires—and to achieve his goals he adjusts to the institution which he joins.[4]

We shall be able to test both propositions for social scientists in industry when we examine the data supplied by them and hear how they made their career choices.

WHEN CAREER CHOICES WERE MADE

It is not surprising that less than a majority of the future Ph.D.s in social science did not have a definite occupational goal in mind when they entered college but we might have assumed that by the time baccalaureate degrees were earned virtually all of the respondents in this study would have selected their occupational goals. As will be shown in the tables below, a third of them had not made a career decision on graduation from college.

Q. Did you have a definite occupational goal in mind:

	Per cent	
	Yes	*No*
Upon entering college?	44	56
Upon completing college?	67	33
During graduate studies?	85	15
On receiving doctorate?	88	12

Averages have a way of covering more detailed breakdowns of data. In this case, let us see if there were any significant differences among the respondents when the data are broken out in terms of the fields of social science they ultimately selected for doctoral studies:

When Occupational Goals Were Determined by Fields of Social Science

	On entering college	*On completing college*	*During grad. studies*	*On receiving doctorate*
Economists	41%	68%	88%	92%
Psychologists	33	63	81	87
Sociologists	61	72	94	94
Statisticians	51	67	72	83

We can see now that there were no really significant differences among the respondents by the time they had completed college studies, and it was then that their ideas as to what kind of career to follow began to firm up. This finding may be of some comfort to parents who worry a great deal about their childrens' future careers, especially high-talent children. There will not be much solace in knowing that their well-meant advice as to courses of study, and other direction for the kind of career the parents want for the child does not carry much weight, at least as far as future social scientists are concerned, as the table below shows:

Q. As you think back to the time when you selected the field in which you earned you doctorate, can you identify any person who played a key role in helping you to choose your career?

Key person	Per cent
College teacher	43
Professional in same field	7
Friend	4
Parent	4
Fellow student	3
Guidance counselor	3
Book on field of study of Ph.D.	*
No one	36
	100

* less than 1 per cent

The rather low rank given to parents as key persons in the process of career choice may be partially explained by the findings of Abraham Jaffe and Walter Adams that children are more realistic than their parents in thinking about education beyond high school. This was true regardless of the occupational grouping of the head of the household of the young persons' families.[5]

Stated occupational goals

Closer study of the goals given by the respondents in this research showed that their choices as to the kind of setting in which they wanted to work were already well formed by the time of receiving the Ph.D., especially in the cases of those who expressed a preference for college teaching or for a career in industry before going on for the doctorate. There was a sizable number, however, who had no question as to the field but who had not decided as to setting. The table below shows the changes in goals from the time of the baccalaureate to completion of doctoral studies:

Comparison of Occupational Goals at B.A./B.S. and Ph.D.

	Economists B.A. B.S.	Ph.D.	Psychologists B.A. B.S.	Ph.D.	Sociologists B.A. B.S.	Ph.D.	Statisticians B.A. B.S.	Ph.D.
College teacher	20%	33%	15%	28%	22%	38%	28%	38%
Industry	18	30	12	26	11	28	11	17
Government	2	2	0	0	0	0	0	0
Non-profit res.	0	2	0	0	0	0	0	0
H.S. teacher	2	0	4	0	5	0	0	0
Another profession	10	0	8	0	17	0	22	0
Same field but setting not determined	16	25	24	33	17	28	6	28
Did not know	32	8	37	13	28	6	33	17
	100	100	100	100	100	100	100	100

TYPOLOGY OF GOALS

From the data above it seems quite clear that by the time of the Ph.D., those who ultimately accepted positions in industry, regardless of earlier beliefs, could be grouped in three occupational goal types:

1. Those who wanted to teach in colleges and universities on completion of doctoral studies;
2. Those who intended to pursue careers in industry; and

3. Those who knew that they wanted to be in the field of their professional training but were uncertain as to the setting in which they would work.

What actually happened

Having seen the typology of goal choices, and the changes that occurred between the baccalaureate and the doctorate, we should now examine—in quantitative terms—what actually happened. In order to have a clearer picture, we need to have two pieces of information about the respondents: (1) Their ages at the time of completion of undergraduate studies, and (2) the number of years between the baccalaureate and the doctorate. These data are shown below:

1. Ages on Graduation from College

Age	Per cent	Cumulative Per cent
18–19	5	
20–21	44	49
22–23	28	77
24–25	22	99
26 or over	1	100

2. Number of Years Between B.A./B.S. and Ph.D.

Years	Per cent	Cumulative Per cent
1–2	1	
3–4	15	16
5–6	22	38
7–8	22	60
9–10	18	78
11–12	13	91
13–14	4	95
15 or more	5	100

There were no significant differences in these data when they were compared by fields of science. We should know, however, before proceeding with our analysis, how the information com-

pared with some other studies of professionals. The most meaningful figure is that showing the number of years between baccalaureate and doctorate, for we should have some idea as to
whether the social scientists in industry were typical or atypical
when compared wth others.

The research selected for comparison with the respondents in
this study was as follows:

1. Sixty-four eminent biologists, social scientists, and physical
   scientists by Anne Roe.[6]
2. A study of Columbia University graduates who achieved distinction as measured by academic awards, fellowships, and
   other honors.[7]
3. A statistical study of the output of doctoral degrees at all U.S.
   universities from 1920 to 1961.[8]

Group Studied	Median years between B.A./B.S. and Ph.D
Social Scientists in Industry	7.5
Columbia University Ph.D.'s in the group	7.5
64 Eminent Scientists	4.3
NAS-NRC study of Doctorate Production	9.8

It should be noted that Anne Roe did her research about
1948, at which time her subjects averaged about forty-eight
years of age. Their education was obviously not affected by
World War II; whereas the subjects in this research and those
included in the Columbia University group were both of military draft age at that time. If one allows a three-year difference
because of the possible interruption by military service of the
education plans of those who went on for the doctorate, then the
first three groups above are remarkably similar with respect to
their ages when the Ph.D. was awarded. Comparison with the
figure in the NAS-NRC study is not meaningful because Ph.D.s
in education were included whose mean span between baccalaureate and doctorate was 14.9 years and thus had a biasing
effect on the over-all median age in the figures reported.

We shall return now to the question "What actually happened?" that is, what gainful employment, if any, was undertaken from college graduation until undertaking doctoral studies and what effect did this have on employment after receiving the Ph.D.? The table below gives us this information.

Comparison of Jobs at Baccalaureate and Doctorate

	All respondents B.A.		Economists B.A.		Psychologists B.A.		Sociologists B.A.		Statisticians B.A.	
	B.S.	Ph.D.	B.S.	Ph.D	B.S.	Ph.D	B.S.	Ph.D	B.S.	Ph.D
	Per cent									
College or univ. teacher	27	32	35	39	18	28	32	33	34	21
Industry	23	50	35	47	18	49	21	38	8	68
Government	9	8	17	8	5	11	5	5	8	11
Non-profit org.	6	10	0	6	7	12	16	24	0	0
H.S. teacher	6	0	3	0	2	0	16	0	8	0
Continued to Ph.D. Not employed full-time	29		10		50		10		42	
	100	100	100	100	100	100	100	100	100	100

The data above reveal quite sharply the direction of movement once the Ph.D. was acquired. It is obvious that the largest accretion was to industry. In this move, statisticians show up very prominently; they were the only ones who left academic life for the industrial world in any sizable number. This change no doubt reflects the demand by industry for highly trained statisticians in the newest fields of data processing and systems analysis.

In the next chapter, we shall be hearing from the respondents the reasons why they accepted positions in industry. Before proceeding to this aspect of the research, we should first listen to a few of the social scientists to gain insight as to how and why they decided on the fields that they selected for doctoral studies.

HOW AND WHY CAREERS IN SOCIAL SCIENCE
WERE DETERMINED

The interviews with the social scientists in industry were usually started with a question along these lines: "Tell me how you happened to follow the kind of career you did. Why did you select the field you are in now for doctoral study?" The verbatim responses which follow are quite representative samples from the research population.

A sociologist, now a member of the technical staff at a research laboratory of a large communications company said:

I thought I wanted to be a C.P.A. so I majored in Accounting at college. After a while, I became dissatisfied with this kind of work but decided to get my degree and get a job in accounting to see how things worked out. As I expected, accounting was not for me. While working, I went to school at night to explore some other fields. I found the courses in Sociology very stimulating. After some conferences with two Sociology professors at Columbia, I decided to quit my job and work for a Ph.D. in Sociology on a full-time basis.

An industrial psychologist, now at an insurance company, also started in accounting. Among his electives, he took a course in psychology and at first found it very boring. "The second semester in that subject turned out to be crucial for me as I was fortunate enough to have an excellent and inspiring teacher who made me realize that Psychology was a vast field for exploration. By the time of my junior year at college, I knew that I wanted to go on in that field."

Another industrial psychologist, now senior vice-president and research director at a world-famous advertising agency, said that he had very vague notions about an occupational goal when he started as an undergraduate at a liberal arts college. "I didn't like this feeling of vagueness but I didn't know what to do about it. Luckily for me, in a Psychology course at Ohio State, I came under the influence of Professor Wherry and became quite excited about Industrial Psychology. I received my Master's degree in one year and, with encouragement from my professors, continued on for the doctorate."

A statistician at an insurance company gave credit to his high school counselor for his choice of a career:

As a result of some tests my guidance counselor recommended that I go in for actuarial science. I found that I could major in this area at Michigan so I applied there and was accepted. Since my family was able to support me, I went on into graduate work in that field. During summer vacations I worked for an insurance company and found that I could put my graduate training to good use, especially if I had the Ph.D. in my field.

An economist for a large oil company said that he thought he wanted to be a corporation lawyer. "I wanted to be a big shot and make a lot of money. However, while in college I became interested in social problems and believed that Economics was one area of study that would help to understand economic conditions. At about my sophomore year I knew that I wanted to go into graduate work. The G.I. Bill made it possible for me to go on to the Ph.D. I found I couldn't do much about social problems as a college teacher so I started looking for a job in Washington and became an economic analyst in the government."

The manager of the planning department in another major oil company explained how he happened to take a Ph.D. in international economics:

I became interested in international affairs while I was an undergraduate in college and wanted to do something about making the world a better place to live in after the war but I didn't quite know how to go about it. I thought of government work but that didn't appeal to me. I decided I had better try to find out more about what goes on outside our own country so I applied for an overseas job with this company and was sent to the Middle East to work in one of their affiliates. By the end of the two-year contract I realized that I had to learn much more about international economics so I decided to go back to school and took graduate work at Johns Hopkins.

Another economist, now in the economics department of a large company, said that because of his middle-class upbringing he developed a social conscience about working people and decided to specialize in labor relations by taking graduate work in that field after completing his undergraduate studies at Princeton. "After getting the M.B.A. at Columbia I tried to get a job in several labor unions," he said, "but I found a lot of suspicion on the part of union people of college graduates who wanted to work for unions. I gave up that notion and ultimately received a Ph.D. in Economics at N. Y. U. with the thought that I might become a college teacher or work for the government."

Two industrial psychologists revealed in their interviews that they became interested in this field as a career as a result of reading books on the subject. One was majoring in physical education with the intention of becoming an athletic coach. He joined the navy at the outbreak of war and was assigned to naval aviation. "When I was assigned as an instructor in pilot training, I became very interested in the learning process and started reading books in Psychology trying to find out what I could about why some people learn faster than others. This interest brought me into contact with some of the Navy's psychologists and they encouraged me to go into the field professionally when the war ended."

The other psychologist majored in languages with the thought that he might enter the foreign service on graduation from college because his uncle was in that branch of government. "By the time I finished college, I had changed my mind and decided to look for a job in Wall Street," he said. "I didn't like this work very much after a while and before I could look for another job, the war broke out. I joined the Navy as a reserve officer and was assigned to the submarine service. During the long patrols, I had plenty of time to read. One of the books I stumbled on was about Industrial Psychology. The subject interested me so much I sent for more books on the subject. By the time the war was over, I knew that I wanted to get into the field of Industrial Psychology."

An economist in a manufacturing company:

I started in college by taking an engineering course but after a while I knew that I wasn't cut out to be an engineer. The war came along and while I was in the Army, I took some correspondence courses in Law and Economics. After the war I went back to school but I had no special career plans. By luck, a college advisor suggested that I major in Economics. I knew that it would be good for me to take graduate work in that field but I wasn't sure I wanted to go all the way to the Ph.D. However, I thought having that degree would be good insurance for the future and so I stayed on in graduate school until I received the doctorate.

Summary and analysis

The interviews with the respondents in this study has confirmed earlier research that there is no pattern of experience that can be developed into a theory of occupational choice by individuals. We have seen that a number of the social scientists believed that accident or luck was the variable that produced changes of direction. At the same time, it is quite obvious that college teachers played a very important part as influencers of young people of college age as to the fields of social science that the respondents selected for doctoral studies. The Columbia research project, earlier mentioned, found that college teachers were quite influential in helping students decide on their careers but not to the same degree as is reported here. The subjects in both groups, however, had made their career decisions by the time of college graduation. Our findings confirm those of other studies that high-talent youngsters select their careers earlier than their contemporaries and, in the main, have done this by the time of college graduation. We should not forget, though, that a third of the social scientists in this study said that they had not made a career decision when they received their bachelors' degrees. If high-talent youngsters have such difficulty and, as has been pointed out, make their career decisions earliest, there is an obvious need for much more research to be done on the determinants of occupational choice.

The finding that over half of the future social scientists had not veered in their occupational goals from the time of the baccalaureate to the doctorate should provide some assurance to the recruiters for industry that there will be highly qualified people available for filling professional jobs in the social sciences. As we shall see in the next chapter, they are not attracted to industry because of pay or fringe benefits but because they feel that industry offers a real opportunity to pursue a professional career. The findings in this chapter also indicate that deans and department heads in colleges and universities cannot assume that the holder of a Ph.D. in one of the social sciences is necessarily headed in the direction of academia. The competition from industry is strong and is likely to become stronger. Attracting high-talent people to accept positions in any setting is only one aspect of the situation; holding them is of far greater importance. The implications for administration of professional personnel will be examined in due course.

Government administrators will have difficulty recruiting social scientists at the doctoral level if the individuals are able to find positions elsewhere. This is not an unalterable situation. A number of government departments have undertaken studies to find out why their recruiting efforts for professionals have not been successful. The findings have not been published, but, in discussions with several knowledgeable people in government and also those who have done the research, it was apparent that salary is not the most important block. As a matter of fact, starting salaries in government are quite comparable to industry and usually better than in colleges and universities. The intrinsic factors—and there are many—far outweigh the extrinsic ones.

We have seen in this chapter that a fair-sized number of highly trained social scientists had not made up their minds as to where they wanted to work after receiving the doctorate. For the most part, they ultimately went to industry to pursue their professional careers. Whether industry can continue to employ most of those whose career plans are not firm at the time of receiving the Ph.D. remains to be seen. With the demand for highly trained social scientists increasing and the supply, relative to population growth, decreasing it is certain that the competition for their services will be very sharp.

We have heard from the respondents why they decided on the fields of social science that took them into graduate studies and finally to a Ph.D. To complete our information on why they selected industry in which to apply their training, we turn to the next chapter to hear from the social scientists their motivations for this choice.

WHY SOCIAL SCIENTISTS ACCEPT POSITIONS IN INDUSTRY

4

If one were to ask a variety of people working in government or non-profit organizations, or faculty members at colleges or universities why their colleagues might leave for positions in industry, the most likely answer would be: "Why? To make more money, of course!" They would be partly right in their assumption that, because industry offers larger salaries than the organizations mentioned above, the primary motivation for a change could be attributed to this cause. As a matter of fact, money is an important motivator in the decision to move to private enterprise but it is not the most important reason, as we shall see after hearing from our respondents. We shall start our investigation by listening in on some of the reasons given during the interviews and some of the write-in comments by the respondents in their replies as to why they accepted their present positions.

WHAT SOME SOCIAL SCIENTISTS SAID ABOUT WHY THEY ENTERED INDUSTRY

The opportunity to do experimental research was the most portant influence on an industrial psychologist who is now director of research in a large advertising agency. He said:

After I obtained my Ph.D. at Michigan, I wanted to come to New York where I felt there would be many interesting problems to work on. I thought about the possibility of teaching and research but that didn't appeal to me. I found a job working for a municipal department involved with juvenile delinquency—that was fine for a while but too limited. Then this job opportunity opened up and I took it because I saw a great opportunity to do large-scale research in my field. I have been able to persuade the company to spend money on experimental research as well as the usual kinds of surveys that we have to do.

A sociologist at the corporate headquarters of a large public utility company, after a few years of teaching at a university, sought a change and explained why:

I wanted to try out some of my ideas in industry and when I heard of an opportunity to get into the personnel department of this company, I took it. I found that there wasn't too much interest in research and when I was offered a job in operations I accepted because I wanted to see what it was like to be a line manager. I must say I liked that kind of work very much but I was persuaded by my present boss to come back to Personnel to start some research on management selection. At first I was dubious that this would be a worth-while change, but he was very persuasive and asked me to at least give it a try. He was right; I'm much more satisfied now being involved in this important research.

An economist at a major oil company became interested in labor unions after graduating from a liberal arts college:

I went to Columbia for an M.B.A. majoring in labor economics but when I tried to find a job in a labor union, I met with little success. . . . I realized that I had to think more realistically if I wanted to support my wife, so I enrolled for a Ph.D. in economics at N.Y.U. at night and worked during the day. I started by working for a small consulting company that did economic research for large corporations. I liked the work but felt exploited. The pay was low and the turnover was high. Eventually, I found a job in the economics department of a competitor company to the one I'm now in but the department was headed by an accountant who had fixed attitudes and was very provincial in his thinking. I stuck it out until I got the Ph.D. and started looking around. When I was interviewed here, I asked a lot of questions about the kind of work I was expected to do. I liked their answers and so I shifted to this company. I must say it was a good move for me. People respect my work and I see it put to good use.

A mathematical statistician at a large research laboratory commented on the question of money and motivation:

My main reason for being here is not salary. I hear rumors that if you work for such-and-such a company, you'd get more money. As far as I'm concerned, I'm well satisfied with the pay and fringe benefits. I'm getting a lot more than I ever expected to get. Some of the people who left for higher salaries in other companies came back because they missed the kind of freedom we have here. There are statisticians in other parts of this company who have asked to be transferred to the lab because they don't have the same kind of freedom as we have here.

An industrial psychologist at an insurance company went directly into an industrial organization when he completed his doctoral work. Explaining why he took this route, he said:

After doing work in industry while working for the Ph.D., it seemed natural for me to continue in industry. I didn't think I could be a good teacher because I wasn't theoretical enough. I left my first job after a few years because I had been in labor relations and didn't like the kind of irrational scheming that went on. In my present job I had an opportunity to become involved in personnel research, a field that appealed to me very much, so I resigned from my first job and came here.

An economist who is a vice-president of a large bank never had any doubt that he would take up a career in industry when his studies were completed:

My family has always had some kind of business and it was very natural for me to think along this line," he said. "I went to Columbia for an M.B.A. and majored in Accounting with a minor in Banking. Columbia put me to work on some statistical problems that involved contact with the chief economist of this bank. I decided that I should go on for the Ph.D. in Economics and, when I received the degree, that chief economist that I had contacted as a student offered me a job. I think of myself as an economist but my economist friends say I am a banker.

An industrial psychologist at a public utility gave a quick reply to the interviewer's question:

Salary, of course! But there really was another reason. I was being pretty well paid working for a consulting company but I never got the feeling of accomplishment. We always had to worry about budgeting time and, as a result, a lot of interesting problems were never fully researched. In my present job, no one pushes me and I have every opportunity to try out my own ideas. When a project is undertaken, I can see it all the way through.

A social psychologist in charge of management development in a multi-plant manufacturing corporation explained how he entered industry and why he took his present job:

When I majored in psychology in college, I thought of myself as becoming a clinician or teaching at a college and doing research in clinical psychology. As I neared the end of my Ph.D. program at Michigan, I was given an offer by a small college to start a psychology department, to be chairman of the department, and have the rank of full professor. I guess I was the youngest full professor on any campus in the country. In time, I became disenchanted with teaching, with the petty administrative details, and the stultified atmosphere of a small provincial college. About this time, a psychological consulting company asked me if I would be interested in working with industrial clients, and I was glad to accept the offer.

After several years at the consulting company, an executive search firm got in touch with me. It seems that one of their clients was looking for a man to head up a new department which would be involved with developing an appraisal system for executives. This seemed to me to be a great challenge and so I accepted. At first I was assigned to the Personnel Director but actually I worked independently. I now have my own department and report to the president.

WRITE-IN COMMENTS

The respondents contacted by letter and questionnaire were asked to reply to this question: "Why did you accept employment with your present organization?" Their replies, not surprisingly, were terse and candid. Later in this chapter, the responses, sorted out into extrinsic and intrinsic categories, will be shown in quantifiable form. At this point the write-in comments will be presented under headings of the several social sciences. Redundancies have been avoided but there will be some repetitiveness in order to retain the flavor of the replies.

By Economists

Salary; more scope for pursuing my interests and ideas.

To vary my experience by working in private industry (Had been in government) and salary.

I felt the company needed me; I respected my boss; the salary was good and so was the location (California).

It offered an opportunity in a growing industry in which I could effectively use my talent.

Challenge of a new position in the company, working directly with top management and with a free hand.

Because it promised to afford me a substantial opportunity to contribute to the shaping of a major business organization's destiny.

To leave unsatisfactory situation at a Southern university. Present job combines good salary, good organization, good location (California), and interesting work.

Loss of enthusiasm for teaching; substantial increase in salary; opportunity to test effectiveness of knowledge.

It offered challenges and research in areas in which I was qualified and interested.

Opportunity to establish a new division conducting research and educational activities in an area of major personal interest.

Opportunity to study for Ph.D. and apply knowledge of economics and investments to investment management.

Opportunity to apply economic knowledge to practical business forecasting; opportunity to write and do research; higher salary than in teaching.

Because of my desire to operate in the business community under conditions of utmost freedom. I was the first person appointed to the position.

Opportunity to earn more money while continuing to engage in research in marketing on a more intensive basis.

More professional, more diversified, security, long-range career possibility, better income.

Strong and competently staffed in my area of interest—corporate public relations.

By Psychologists

Greater challenge; tougher personnel problems and more willing to work on them.

Opportunity to do significant, long-term research in my area of interest. Organization is receptive to application of findings from psychological research.

Established and well known industrial psychologist was to be my supervisor.

Because it afforded me better research opportunities than alternative employment.

I wanted to cut down on travel. (Had been with a management consultant company.)

Money; opportunity for advancement; freedom to explore and learn more about my field and to use electronic data processing.

Good laboratory situation; improvement over academic salary.

Affiliation with the social science research unit seemed like an opportunity I could not afford to miss.

Wanted more operational work, to work on immediate management problems.

Dissatisfaction with university; had a consulting relationship while teaching; challenging opportunity with plenty of management support.

Looked attractive as emphasis seemed to be on basic research; good salary; bright and imaginative associates.

To have full responsibility for development of big simulation program to be used for training and research purposes. Salary increase.

Discovered during post-doctorate years that opportunity, challenge and excitement were to be found in the corporate arena.

Opportunity for mixture of personnel research and personnel management.

To spend more time in Research and Development. For some time I had been doing more and more managing and less and less research.

Great opportunity to work in an area and organization wanting and needing what I had to offer.

By Sociologists

A former client of mine without a personnel department asked me to establish one and work for that company exclusively.

Opportunities for growth both personal and within the company were greater than in government service.

Seemed to offer the best opportunity without losing sight of long-range goal and without too much compromise.

Opportunity to set up my own department in an exceptionally fast growing, creative advertising agency.

Chance for research and for application of research knowledge.

Because of financial, learning, and career opportunities.

Better salary; new and interesting ideas.

It seemed to present an opportunity to become acquainted with and develop research skills in a heretofore little explored area: human group-complex machine interface. In addition, I was attracted by what seemed to be a much more flexible work situation, more professional freedom and, of course, a markedly superior salary.

The challenge as well as the organization mission which permits me to use my academic training.

To have full responsibility for development of a big simulation program. Salary increase.

I became disillusioned and unhappy teaching.

Keen interest in company and product combined with an opportunity to make a contribution.

Interesting technically; international in purpose; money.

Opportunity for challenging work; ability to do research in "real life" setting; salary.

By Statisticians

With only a B.A. in 1957, I didn't have much choice. Then, when I received the Ph.D. in 1964, I returned to industry because I

thought I would have a good opportunity to pursue more exciting problems.

Prior to my completing my Ph.D. work, I returned to industry to
get experience and, since I was married, also to assist my bank
account which was nearly depleted.

Because I would get a good opportunity to do research which I
thought would be useful to human beings and at the same time
acquire more knowledge.

Seemed to be a good place to do my kind of research.

Compatibility with colleagues; interesting problems.

Challenge of diversified problems; intelligent, capable colleagues.
An atmosphere of high horsepower.

Geography was the deciding factor among several jobs of equal opportunity; also, extra freedom.

More authority; more money.

Opportunity to do applied research in mathematical statistics and
to use computers.

Provided an opportunity to establish a new organization for mathematics and statistics within a progressively managed company.

Opportunity for learning from more knowledgeable associates and
for working on interesting applied problems.

Opportunity in a fast growing industry and freedom to pursue a
scientific career.

I was assured that I would have the opportunity to carry out my
own research work.

The reader has, by now, gained a number of impressions that
seem to run throughout all of the comments. Opportunity, challenge, starting a new department, freedom to do research to his
liking and, of course, money were all emphasized. In order to
determine which factors had the most weight in the decision to
accept positions in industry, all of the replies were tabulated
and grouped under two main headings and further broken
down under each heading as follows:

1. *Extrinsic*, that is, salary, fringe benefits, geographical location,
   and other material benefits.
2. *Intrinsic*, that is, challenging work, freedom to do research,
   interesting problems, and the like, and loss of interest in
   teaching.

The two tables shown below will be in percentage terms but will add up to more than 100 per cent because every respondent gave more than one reason. The first table will be related to the separate social sciences and the second to the last place of employment, if any, before joining his present organization. Thus, we shall be able to determine whether the reasons given by economists, for example, are the same or different from those given by sociologists. After probing the factors associated with the separate sciences, we will want to know whether the variable of previous employment was an important factor in reply to the question "Why did you accept employment with your present organization?"

Reasons for Accepting Employment with Present Organization and Field of Social Science

	Per cent				
Reasons	All respon-dents	Econo-mists	Psychol-ogists	Sociol-ogists	Statis-ticians
EXTRINSIC:					
Salary	46	48	50	43	37
Good job opportunity	25	33	22	29	11
Location	8	8	10	0	16
INTRINSIC:					
To use Ph.D. training as a scientist	67	60	78	62	63
Challenging work	30	33	26	29	26
Prestige of company, superiors, or associates	18	10	24	15	32
Interest and variety of research	16	13	18	15	32
Free to try own ideas	10	4	2	24	16
Lost interest in teaching at college or university	2	3	1	1	0

The fact that two-thirds or more of the respondents felt that work in industry would afford them an excellent opportunity to use their Ph.D. training more fully than in non-industrial settings, regardless of the field of social science, is at variance with some generalizations about scientists in industry. If there is "conflict and accommodation"—a phrase used by William Kornhauser as a subtitle to his book on industrial scientists[1]—then it should follow that social scientists would be reluctant to accept positions in industry or, having experienced this kind of life, should have left to pursue their desires for self-fulfillment in non-commercial organizations. There *are* stresses and strains for the professional social scientist in industry; their nature will be seen in the next chapter. At this point, however, it seemed clear that the respondents believed that the industrial world offered many intrinsic as well as extrinsic attractions for a fruitful career.

Assuming that private industry does attract highly trained scientists, an obvious question should be raised at this point: do they stay? The answer to this question is contained in the data of the next table:

Years Served in Present Position and Field of Social Science

Years	Per cent			
	Economists	*Psychologists*	*Sociologists*	*Statisticians*
Less than 3	9	8	11	15
3 to 6	39	40	22	35
7 to 10	26	30	33	40
11 to 15	16	15	17	10
15 to 19	4	5	11	0
20 and over	6	2	6	0
	100	100	100	100
Less than 3 years	9	8	11	15
3 years or more	91	92	89	85

The typical faculty appointment is for three years before tenure is granted. In government or non-profit organizations, top management usually decides within a three-year period if an employee, especially a highly paid one, should be retained or encouraged to resign. As for the individual professionals, the market demand for their services is so strong that any fear of unemployment must be practically nonexistent. The fact that such a large percentage of social scientists have chosen to remain in their present organizations speaks for itself.

We have heard from the respondents why they accepted their present positions in industry. We now know that a very large majority of them, in all of the social sciences, stay in their present organizations once having joined them. What are some of the factors that provide the satisfactions for such highly trained individuals that keep them interested? Are there any major dissatisfactions? We turn now to these questions in the next chapter.

ATTITUDES OF INDUSTRIAL SOCIAL SCIENTISTS TOWARD THEIR WORK; COMPARISON WITH ATTITUDES OF PHYSICAL SCIENTISTS IN INDUSTRY

5

In this chapter we shall be examining the answers from social scientists on questions related to various aspects of their work and, at the same time, making direct comparisons with the responses of their colleagues in the physical sciences on the same questions. As stated earlier, the comprehensive research undertaken by Donald Pelz and Frank Andrews was one of the few studies that separated the replies of those with doctorates from the rest of their research population. This made it possible to compare the responses to a number of questions addressed to scientists with equal levels of high-level training in both the social and physical sciences. Such a comparison should throw some light on whether the findings of various writers on "scientists" can be applied generally, or if there are differences because of field of science, level of training, or other factors.

Sir Charles Snow coined the phrase "two cultures" to suggest a wide gulf between the beliefs, opinions, and philosophies of physical scientists and of those he described as "literary intellectuals," among whom he included social scientists.[1] Lewis Terman, in his longitudinal study of gifted children, found that when the children became adults, those who had majored in the social sciences and humanities "were at opposite poles" from the physical scientists in occupational interests and behavior.[2] Anne Roe said that the characteristic pattern among physical scientists was that of shy, lonely, overintellectualized individuals; whereas the social scientists were very active in social affairs and were frequently "big shots" in college. "This contrast was still evident after they grew up," she wrote.[3]

It is not within the realm of this study to explore the matter of "differences" psychologically between the two types of scientists. We shall, however, be looking through their eyes at their worlds of work and listening to their comments and reactions and to the reports of those who have explored these worlds. If there are significant differences between social scientists and physical scientists in industry, by the end of this chapter we should be able to "see" them.

WHAT SOME WRITERS HAVE FOUND

The most frequently voiced observation of those who have studied scientists at work in industry is that there is a conflict between the management mind and the scientific mind. Robert Anthony stated the problem succinctly when he wrote:

The professional employee of an organization is subject to two often conflicting sets of expectations, demands, and identifications. The fact that he is a member of a profession constrains him to act according to the standards set by the profession rather than by the work of the establishment. He has obligations to the profession to maintain these standards in the face of conflicting demands the establishment may make on him. His special competence is not fully at the disposal of his employer. Organizations limit professionals, for organizations strive to mobilize professional people to serve their own ends, and to organize professional people along their own lines.[4]

A writer for the *Wall Street Journal*, after interviewing management people in a number of industrial research laboratories, came to the conclusion that "scientists are a different breed of men than the usual employee. Scientists, personnel men say, bring to the world of business fixed attitudes on everything from profits to proper attire, attitudes that often clash head on with those of management."[5] Mark Abrahamson believes that the adjustment of scientists to industrial settings is most difficult when the scientist has extensive graduate training, strong demands for autonomy, and a desire to engage in basic research.[6] Simon Marcson found in his study of scientists in industry that the professional employee develops a resistance to domination by executive authority especially if its source is non-professional. "A scientist's training does not ready him for a position in industry as an employee," wrote Marcson.[7]

We shall, in due course, see whether social scientists should be included in descriptions and characterizations such as those cited, as we compare the responses of the social scientists and physical scientists to certain aspects of their work in industry.

THE WORLD OF THE SOCIAL SCIENTIST IN INDUSTRY

To begin our exploration, we need some data for a frame of reference. In what kinds of companies do social scientists work, and at what level in the management hierarchy in the various types of enterprises? The tables below furnish these data:

Types of Organizations and Field of Science of Respondents

	Per cent			
	Economists	*Psychologists*	*Sociologists*	*Statisticians*
Manufacturing	48	43	50	44
Service	16	18	25	4
Finance	27	11	5	4
Public Utilities	9	10	15	0
Research lab.	0	18	5	48
	100	100	100	100

Types of Organizations and Level in Management of Respondents

	Per cent			
	Top Management	Middle Management	Bottom Management	Total
Manufacturing	21	38	41	100
Service	57	29	14	100
Finance	41	44	15	100
Public utilities	7	40	53	100
Research lab.	0	30	70	100

We see from the first table that the distribution of social scientists among the various types of companies is about what one might have expected except that it was somewhat surprising to find an absence of Ph.D. statisticians in public utility companies where electronic data processing is used quite extensively.

The second table holds more significance for our later analysis. If we combine the percentages of social scientists in top and middle management positions, it can be seen that, except for research laboratories, such scientists are to be found in responsible staff positions in management. This is especially true in service and finance companies where top management policy decisions lean heavily on social science research results.

The finding that social scientists are in important staff positions in their organizations exposes one major difference in the work world of the physical and social scientists; most of the former are to be found in research laboratories far removed geographically and hierarchically from corporate headquarters. The research that has been carried out on physical scientists has, in almost all cases, been confined to "bench scientists" in research laboratories. This is a major variable to consider as we begin our exploration of scientists at work.

AUTONOMY

To most writers on the subject of scientists in industry, the aspect given first attention is autonomy. Robert Anthony defined autonomy as "freedom from strict supervision, freedom to plan details of his work, freedom to discuss his work with his colleagues and superiors, freedom to publish technical papers, and especially freedom to spend a part of his time working on ideas which are completely unrelated to his assigned work."[8] Much of Anthony's definition is implied in the question that follows:

Q. Concerning your own work or the work you supervise, to what extent do you have autonomy to determine your own technical programs—in contrast to having work assigned or suggested by higher level of supervisors, managers, customers, clients, etc.?

Amount of Autonomy	Per cent				
	Physical Scientists	Econo- mists	Psychol- ogists	ogists Sociol-	Statis- ticians
Nil to moderate	36	19	33	18	21
Substantial	57	61	53	41	58
Complete	7	20	14	41	21
	100	100	100	100	100

Autonomy and Position Level of Social Scientists

	Top Management	Middle Management	Bottom Management
Nil to moderate	12	16	44
Substantial	60	61	46
Complete	28	23	10
	100	100	100

Autonomy and Type of Organization

	Manufacturing	Finance	Service	Public Utility	Research Lab.
Nil to mooderate	25	16	21	18	41
Substantial	56	64	49	73	42
Complete	19	20	30	9	16
	100	100	100	100	100

The statistical data on autonomy show that most social scientists in this study, especially the sociologists, have a somewhat greater amount of autonomy than do the industrial physical scientists. However, in general, both types have a substantial amount of freedom in their work. Social scientists in research laboratories come closest to the feelings of physical scientists. This is understandable, for it is not likely that social scientists, working under similar conditions, would be given more autonomy than their colleagues in the physical sciences.

It is of some significance that social scientists in middle management report as much autonomy as those in top management. In most organizations, the professional is placed in an important staff position because the higher management feels the need of expert advice in the social scientist's specialty. There would not be much sense in telling a professional how to perform his work in a field for which he was highly trained. As John Galbraith noted in his *New Industrial State,* organized knowledge can be brought to bear, not surprisingly, only by those who possess it.

When we analyze the data on autonomy by types of organizations, we find—by combining "substantial" and "complete"— that, except for those in research laboratories, three-quarters or more of the social scientists felt that they had considerable autonomy.

The inference made by some writers that industrial scientists do not have enough autonomy does not hold for social scientists. As a matter of fact, the Pelz-Andrews data show that two-thirds of the Ph.D. scientists and engineers do not share this feeling either.

HOW MANAGERS OF SCIENTISTS VIEW AUTONOMY

Although management people know from studies that have been reported that the need for autonomy is strongly emphasized by their scientific employees, the reactions of managers are sometimes laced with a kind of resentment that is best illustrated by two examples taken from interviews with those in charge of research for their companies. The first comes from a general survey carried out by Opinion Research Corporation:

I feel that the freedom often referred to is actually a form of laziness. Too many people want to do what they want, when they want, and how they want with no regard to the over-all effect this has on the company. The place for such freedom is in academic institutions, not competitive industry.[9]

The next quote is from a manager of a research laboratory of a chemical products company:

How can I get these independent characters to see that they have to operate within the organization and that corporate needs are sometimes more important than requirements of the scientific method? They don't really understand what we are in business for, and every time I try to pin them down to do something for the company, they run off to another meeting where they can read highbrow papers and get their egos inflated.[10]

At a conference conducted by the Foundation for Research on Human Behavior, one of the panelists decried the attitudes of newly recruited social scientists who come into industry. "Some young social scientists who have recently completed their Ph.D.s appear to enter industry waving their degrees like witch doctors brandishing their magic wands, lacking humility, and thereby alienating many businessmen."[11]

A check on how the respondents in this study reacted to statements attributed to scientists in industry was made possible by extracting statements from some studies[12] and asking the social scientists to react to them by indicating agreement or disagreement, and to add written comments if they wished. The first of these related to autonomy:

The scientist is aware of the corporation's goals but at the same time he wants autonomy. His goals involve research unrestricted by managerial assignment or marketing demands.

Below are the responses shown in quantitative form. These data will be followed by some of the write-in comments.

	Per cent			
	Agree	Disagree	Undecided	Total
Economists	30	59	11	100
Psychologists	38	55	7	100
Sociologists	22	61	18	100
Statisticians	24	65	11	100

It is obvious that most of the social scientists in this study could not accept the statement. One interpretation of their disagreement could be that their goals *are* restricted by managerial assignment or marketing demands. Another could be read as awareness of management's goals and the social scientist's willingness to tackle problems posed by management; that undertaking such research does not create conflict with his own goals. Our understanding of the data above may be assisted by reading some of the comments that accompanied the check marks on the questionnaire.

WRITE-IN COMMENTS

The director of marketing planning for a manufacturing company disagreed with the statement and explained why: "This statement is particularly untrue for an economist. There is a good overlap of objectives."

A staff economist in an advertising agency also disagreed and added: "Although I recognize the desirability and long-range advantages of 'pure research,' I like to see a payoff in reasonably expeditious applications. I'm sure that this 'practical bent' of mine was a disappointment to at least one member of my Ph.D. committee when I took my orals."

The manager of research development at an advertising agency, an industrial psychologist, agreed and wrote: "The statement is very true and requires some sympathetic give and take on both sides. Scientists, acting autonomously, may know better than company management what the company needs—but if this compromise cannot work out realistically, the scientist had better get out of the company. He could work for a firm that wants a scientist just for 'window dressing' or for the sake of playing the game of 'forward-looking company'—but this can put him into a much worse environment."

A psychologist on the technical staff of a research laboratory remarked: "There is some element of truth in the statement but it is too extreme. In my company, a scientist with that attitude wouldn't last long."

Another psychologist on the technical staff of a communications research laboratory disagreed with the statement and wrote: "There are scientists and scientists. Some want to do assignment work and do it with great imagination and creativity."

A statistician at the same laboratory disagreed with some vehemence: "Baloney! This characterizes a 'scientist' as one engaged in defrauding the stockholders or clients."

We can summarize the feelings of the social scientists on the question of autonomy as being largely in disagreement with the notion that they are restricted in their freedom to carry out their research in the ways that they believe necessary. They recognize that they have an obligation to the enterprise but see no conflict between their own professional goals and those of the company for which they work. On the basis of the data presented here, and implemented by the write-in comments, it is fair to conclude that social scientists in industry have a high degree of autonomy in their work.

COMMUNICATING IDEAS TO MANAGEMENT

The manager's world is a world of words. Much, perhaps most, of his time is spent in communicating with those about him. Therefore, in order for a social scientist to be effective in a company, he must be able to communicate his ideas to those who either ask for his help or to those that he thinks ought to hear his ideas. How do social scientists in industry feel about this aspect of their work? The next table, to be followed by write-in comments, should provide the necessary information to answer the questions on the problem of communications.

Q. When new and important ideas about your work occur to you, how easily can you get them across to other people who might be interested in or affected by them?

Ease of communicating	Per cent				
	Physical Scientists	Econo-mists	Psychol-ogists	Sociol-ogists	Statis-ticians
Difficult to mixed	29	36	38	13	43
Fairly easy	50	42	40	59	26
Very easy	21	22	22	28	21
	100	100	100	100	100

It is apparent that, except for statisticians, social scientists and physical scientists find it fairly easy or very easy to communicate their ideas to those who might be interested in or affected by them. Before commenting further, it may be useful to rearrange the data in two more ways: by level in management, and by types of organizations, to see whether either of these factors gives us the same or different results as those shown above.

Ease of Communicating New Ideas and Position Level of Social Scientists

	Per cent		
	Top Management	*Middle Management*	*Bottom Management*
Difficult to mixed	28	28	51
Fairly easy	37	47	40
Very easy	35	25	9
	100	100	100

The results above are not unexpected. Those in higher staff management have the job of "translating" their findings to the decision makers. In order to be effective, they learn to use less technical jargon and put their information into familiar terms used in the organization. They are frequently called upon to justify starting research projects and must be able to estimate costs and persuade those at top levels that the research is a worth-while investment for the company. They are also expected to use good judgment in deciding when a research project should be dropped.

The social scientists in bottom management have few of the problems of their hierarchical superiors. They do not always "see" the results of their work put to use. They have the normal reactions of people in bureaucratic organizations who cannot understand why their bright ideas are not immediately adopted or more leeway given to them to carry on research in their own way or for a long enough time to satisfy the researcher, especially at a time when the organization is cutting costs for reasons not always clear to those at the bottom.

To what extent is the problem of communicating new ideas affected by the type of organization in which the social scientist is employed? The next table should give us some data to reply to the question.

Ease of Communicating New Ideas and Type of Organization

	Per cent				
	Manufacturing	Finance	Service	Public Utilities	Research Lab.
Difficult to mixed	34	30	30	30	63
Fairly easy	49	44	40	60	26
Very easy	17	26	30	10	11
	100	100	100	100	100

The most significant figure in the data above tells us that social scientists in research laboratories obviously have problems in communicating their ideas either to upper management or to colleagues in the physical sciences. The problem for the few social scientists in most research laboratories—especially those in manufacturing companies—may result from the fact that most laboratory directors are physical scientists and do not "talk" the same language as is used in the social sciences. Another cause could stem from the observation made by Robert Anthony that the research director has usually had technical training but has rarely reached the top in the laboratory principally because of the brilliance of his technical work. "More commonly," wrote Anthony, "he has been given his job because of his executive ability rather than because he has a record of outstanding technical accomplishment."[13]

Closely associated with the problem of social scientists communicating new ideas to higher management is that of persuading the decision makers that research money should be spent on the proposal. The non-professionals in executive ranks sometimes take a dim view of research proposals and the inevitable result is tension. In this connection, two statements from studies of scientists in industry were included in the questionnaire and the respondents were asked to agree or disagree with them, and to make additional comments if they so desired. The statements and the amount of agreement or disagreement follow together with the write-in comments.

The trouble with many research people is that they go ahead and do research without any appreciation of the cost.

	Per cent			
	Agree	Disagree	Undecided	Total
Economists	41	44	15	100
Psychologists	34	62	4	100
Sociologists	28	50	22	100
Statisticians	24	71	5	100

It was interesting that all of the written comments were made only by those who agreed with the statement.

A department head in the economics department of an oil company agreed but added, "I think the statement is incomplete and should have added to it 'relative to the gain to be realized.' "

Another economist, director of marketing planning for a manufacturing company, commented: "Management looks to good professional people for judgments involving the balancing of cost of research against the value of research in terms of the company's objectives."

A psychologist who is manager of organization planning for an oil company wrote that "the real problem is their lack of appreciation of the value or lack of value of the research they want to do."

A sociologist on the technical staff of a communications company research laboratory commented, "I agree that they go ahead but disagree that it is trouble."

The next statement is also related to the problem of communicating:

Though management theoretically must make decisions as to whether projects should be continued or dropped, in actual practice research programs are dropped largely on the decision of the individual scientists and seldom at the request of management.

Since social scientists in industry are, for the most part, in important staff management positions, the responses will also be shown by levels of management to see how this factor is involved in reacting to the above statement. First, we shall see whether there were any differences in responses by reason of field of social science:

	Per cent		
	Agree	Disagree	Undecided
Economists	30	59	11
Psychologists	38	55	7
Sociologists	22	61	17
Statisticians	24	65	11

Again, we find that social scientists do not accept some of the generalizations attributed to highly trained people in industry.

There are really no significant statistical differences in the reactions to the statement above, but it is of some interest that the widest difference occurs between psychologists and sociologists, the two sciences that are often working on similar problems. It should be noted, however, that the largest percentage of those who could not decide were sociologists. If their reactions had been split evenly between agreement and disagreement, the statistics for sociologists would have been the same as for the other social scientists. This supposition is not being made. Instead, it will be of greater significance to view the data in relation to levels in the management, for we know from previous information that the majority of sociologists were almost all in middle or top management positions in their organizations.

Position in Management and Belief that Social Scientist Decides on Continuing or Stopping Research

	Per cent			
	Agree	Disagree	Undecided	Total
Top Management	27	61	12	100
Middle Management	27	63	10	100
Bottom Management	37	52	11	100

Apparently position in management does not affect the reactions of the social scientists in industry to a significant degree when the question of starting or stopping research is concerned. What the data show is that they see the problem as they do other problems of the enterprise—in terms of value to the organization's goals. Furthermore, the experienced social scientist understands the position of the line manager. He knows that high-level decisions about research budgets are made on an objective basis. A turn-down of a project is not caused by feelings of mistrust or lack of confidence in the scientist's ability. Top managers have "bosses" too—outside directors, stockholders, and customers who strongly influence managerial decisions. Just as the scientist wants his boss to be supportive when he has great enthusiasm for a research project which he is eager to do because of his intense interest in his profession, his boss wants the scientist to understand the organization's problems and accept his decision when it is negative.

WORK INVOLVEMENT

We know from data shown in an earlier chapter that social scientists accepted positions in industry because they believed that this area of activity offered a promising career for applying the intense training they undertook for their doctorates. To what extent did the social scientists find that initial beliefs had been realized? A question was asked to bring out this aspect of their feelings:

Q. Some individuals are completely involved in their technical work—absorbed by it night and day. For others, their work is simply one of several interests. How involved do you feel in your work?

The intensity of feeling of economists, psychologists, and sociologists about their professional involvement stands in sharp contrast to the physical scientists. The statisticians reacted to

	Per cent				
	Physical Scientists	Econo- mists	Psychol- ogists	Sociol- ogists	Statis- ticians
Not much, slightly, or moderately	36	10	16	18	21
Strongly	43	35	34	24	47
Very strongly, completely	21	55	50	58	32
	100	100	100	100	100

this question in about the same way as the physical scientists. As we go on to other aspects, the reader will soon note that statisticians seem to react much more like the physical scientists than their colleagues in the social sciences. As has been previously indicated, the majority of statisticians in this study were located in research laboratories where the physical sciences are dominant in the typical laboratory of private enterprise organizations. It can be assumed that common surroundings will generally produce similar reactions on the kinds of questions being asked here. We can test this assumption by relating work involvement to type of organizations:

Work Involvement and Type of Organization of Social Scientists

	Per cent				
	Manufacturing	Finance	Service	Public Utilities	Research Lab.
Not much, slightly or moderately	12	17	12	20	21
Strongly	34	25	40	40	47
Very strongly, completely	54	68	48	40	32
	100	100	100	100	100

The data above support the earlier contention about similarity of feelings between physical scientists and statisticians— most of whom work in research laboratories. What was not expected was the high intensity of feeling of work involvement of those in banks, insurance companies, and investment houses. The stereotype of the men in financial affairs is a picture of conservative, tradition-bound, facts-and-figures kind of people while that of the white-coated scientist in his laboratory is usually shown to be a man in his proper world of exciting experimentation in the pursuit of knowledge. The last table gives quite a different picture of social scientists in industry. Obviously, type of organization is an important factor in assessing the feelings of work involvement of industrial social scientists.

SELF-PERCEPTIONS OF IMPORTANCE OF THEIR WORK

A primary function of professionalism is the protection of standards of excellence in a profession, guarding against pressure from vested interests for quick solutions to complex problems and "using" the professional for materialistic or political advantage. Academicians assert that the university is the guardian against special interests who are trying to exploit the work of the scientist. For example, Wilbert Moore, when he was chairman of the sociology department at Princeton, wrote in 1947:

Whatever the role of the staff specialist in management or trade union, the researcher in the college or university has at least a moderate insulation from the demands of special interests. He occupies a position that affords and in a modest way even encourages what may be called 'strategic neutrality' on policy issues. If he abandons it for exclusive service to any interest group, there is no one who can be certainly counted on for disinterested inquiry.[14]

Loren Baritz, a sociology professor at Wesleyan University, was quite explicit in his feeling that social scientists in industry were exploited:

Managers have the power to hire and fire social scientists. If a social scientist is to be kept on the payroll, he has to produce. The judge of whether he is producing is his boss. Thus industrial social scientists have usually been doing what they are told to do and doing it well . . . endangering those other personal, group, class, and institutional interests which were opposed to domination by the modern corporation of the mood and direction of American life. Endangered most have been the millions of workers who have been forced or seduced into submission to the ministrations of industrial social scientists . . . and the industrial social scientists have been especially willing.[15]

Other voices have been raised to accuse modern-day scientists of losing their professional virtues such as Norbert Weiner's stinging accusation that scientists working on government contracts in industry were "mere stooges in science factories,"[16] or Lewis Feur's belief that the scientific intellectual in the twentieth century has allowed himself to be pushed into a philosophy of torment and despair as his work has become institutionalized and bureaucratized and "he has surrendered the optimistic self-dedication which characterized his predecessors . . . and now advocates no new philosophy but shares the prevalent ideology and values.[17]

Abram Chayes leveled his scorn at scientists in industry when he wrote:

The neglect of basic research, the dilution of the college degree, the organization man, the dullness and superficiality of the mass media, the level of political morality—all these off-spring, wanted or unwanted, find their way in the end to the doorstep of the modern corporation.[18]

How do scientists in industry feel about such rhetoric? Do they see themselves merely as employees on a payroll doing the bidding of their employers, or are there opportunities to add to knowledge, both theoretical and applied, in their fields?

The next question, derived from the Pelz-Andrews study, gives us the opportunity to see how both the physical scientists and social scientists look upon this aspect of their work as professionals in industry. We shall also be able to statistically compare the two types of scientists regarding their feelings about scientific contributions in their fields.

Q. How important do you personally feel your present technical work is—that is, how much of a contribution is it likely to make either to technical knowledge or to practical application, or by other standards?

	Per cent				
Felt importance of work	*Physical Scientists*	*Econo- mists*	*Psychol- ogists*	*Sociol- ogists*	*Statis- ticians*
Of no, slight or moderate importance	21	24	19	38	32
Substantial	36	41	32	24	36
Very substantial utmost	43	35	49	24	36
	100	100	100	100	100

Except for the sociologists, no less than two-thirds of the social scientists and physical scientists feel that they are making substantial contributions to knowledge in their fields. These data reflect quite a different picture than that given by some writers on this aspect of professional work in industry.

PERFORMANCE APPRAISALS

The subject of appraising the worth of individuals for such administrative decisions as promotions, salary increases, change in assignments, and the like, has been the subject of lively controversy for many years. Organizations have concocted all kinds of forms to assist supervisors and personnel administrators to make judgments on employees. Graphic rating scales, the "critical incident" method, "forced choice," and other approaches have been tried. Some research has been undertaken by the larger companies and, in every case, the crucial weakness in validating quantified reports on performance has been criterion. In other words, if the company's management knows what it wants to measure in respect to an individual's performance, it may be possible to create valid forms that will be reasonably objective; there should be a strong correlation between a "score" obtained by quantifying the form and the criterion or criteria expressed in numbers. Some progress has been made but most companies are still looking for easy and convenient ways of measuring performance. When this difficult administrative problem is applied to scientists and engineers, the professional employees generally express resentment and skepticism that they are being fairly judged.

Douglas McGregor observed that in this area of management it is essential to arrange matters organizationally so that people can achieve their own goals that are in consonance with the organization's objectives. He suggested that managements should consider using a new approach to appraise individual performance, a method that involves "management by objectives." "This plan," he wrote, "shifts the emphasis from appraisal to self-analysis and from focus on the past to the future; the subordinate is helped in relating his career planning to the needs and realities of the organization through consultations with his superior."[19] The validity of McGregor's belief, insofar as it may apply to scientists in industry, was tested in this study by posing a question taken from the Pelz-Andrews questionnaire to physical scientists to obtain and compare the reactions of social scientists to this important aspect of personnel administration of highly trained people:

> Q. For each of the following persons or units, how important is it to you that you appear well in their eyes—that you maintain their good opinion of your performance?

NOTE: The numbers in each column are the
weighted averages obtained by the
following scoring system:

	None-o	Slight-1	Moderate-2	Great-3	Utmost-4
Person or Unit	*Physical Scientists*	*Econo- mists*	*Psychol- ogists*	*Sociol- ogists*	*Statis- ticians*
Immediate supervisor	2.86	3.16	3.05	2.94	2.89
Professional col- leagues within R. & D.	2.81	2.47	2.39	2.64	2.62
Higher super- visors within R. & D.	2.69	2.35	2.53	2.27	2.72
Professional col- leagues else- where in the field	2.35	2.29	2.56	2.28	2.61
Top executives within the company	2.00	3.24	2.40	3.00	1.89
Customers or other non- technical de- partments using research	1.25	2.83	2.62	2.44	2.50
Myself	3.71	3.63	3.38	3.53	3.63

The fact that both the social scientists and the physical scientists felt very strongly that they were the best judges of their
work was not surprising. This finding could be dismissed as an
egocentric expression by those who do not realize that the
reaction results from a passionate belief on the part of highly
trained people that they know when they have done a good job
(or a bad one) in their work. Over and over were heard, during
the interviews, such expressions as: "The work has to satisfy me
before I will present any of it to management," or, "regardless
of the pressure put on me for quick results, I insist on maintain-
ing professional standards in our work." Self-analysis, then, is
the key, as was pointed out by McGregor.

Leonard Silk confirmed this finding when he wrote that the scientist's conception of his role is that he is the intellectual equal of anybody, regardless of rank, status, or seniority. His concern for the inviolateness of his intellectual honor is likely to be very intense.[20] Although Silk was writing about physical scientists in research laboratories, it is very clear from the data above that social scientists are equally intense in their loyalties to scientific truth and their own consciences.

There are two aspects of appraisal where social scientists and physical scientists differ, and that is in the feelings they have about the opinions of their work by top executives in the company, and customers or non-technical departments using their work. The very low score given to the latters' opinions is in marked contrast to the reactions of the social scientists toward customers or other departments in the organization. As for the top executives of the company, the physical scientists seem to show little concern for their opinions, whereas the economists and sociologists obviously want to appear well in their eyes. This finding is not hard to understand if the reader will recall that economists and sociologists were more frequently found in top management than psychologists or statisticians. Physical scientists, usually working in research laboratories, are far removed from corporate headquarters; they have little contact with top executives. The opposite is true of social scientists; they are in close communication with the decision makers of the company's affairs.

Both the physical scientists and social scientists do not seem to be greatly concerned about how they appear in the eyes of professional colleagues elsewhere than in their own companies. They are much more concerned about the opinions of their immediate supervisors of their work. This finding raises an important question about the applicability to Ph.D. scientists of statements such as this one:

The professional employee does not look to the formal management structure for meaningful approval or disapproval of his work. His standing as a competent professional cannot be validated by members of his organization, since they are not knowledgeable enough about it. For these reasons, the expert is more likely than others to esteem the good opinions of professional peers elsewhere; he is disposed to seek recognition and acceptance from outsiders.[21]

There is little doubt that both social scientists and physical scientists pay some attention to the opinions of colleagues in their field outside their own organization but not nearly as much as suggested in the above statement or others like it. The variable which has not always been taken into account when making statements about "scientists" is that there are, as Donald Pelz and Frank Andrews reported, noticeable differences between Ph.D.'s and non-Ph.D.'s in their motivations, and quality and quantity of output. "Non-doctoral scientists in Ph.D. dominated laboratories," wrote Pelz and Andrews, "tended to be permanently subordinate. They felt they had less autonomy and influence than other non-doctorals. They saw their professional opportunities as more limited, and they seldom held jobs above middle status."[22]

Does position in the managerial hierarchy affect the feelings of social scientists in industry with regard to the opinions of others about their work? The next table provides the answer to this question:

Importance of Opinions About Performance and Management Level

NOTE: The same scoring system as in the last table was used in obtaining weighted averages.

Person or unit	Top Management	Middle Management	Bottom Management
Myself	3.58	3.59	3.59
Immediate supervisor	3.50	3.13	2.89
Top executives within the co.	3.24	3.08	2.02
Professional colleagues in R. & D.	2.94	2.84	2.39
Customers or other non-technical depts.	2.81	2.31	2.39
Professional colleagues elsewhere in the field	2.43	2.11	2.35

The picture regarding others' opinion about their work becomes even clearer as we analyze the data above. Again we see that top and middle management people in staff positions have strikingly similar views on this aspect as well as others that have been examined. Those in bottom management react much more like the physical scientists. Particular attention should be given to the fact that, regardless of position level, professional colleagues elsewhere in the field were ranked last in the esteem list.

ATTITUDES TOWARD ORGANIZATION RULES AND REGULATIONS

It should not be surprising to find that all scientists chafe when they are hobbled by organization rules and regulations. This should be expected whenever we deal with highly talented and creative people. The tension that sometimes develops between professionals and those who make the rules was well illustrated by a *Wall Street Journal* front-page article under the heading "Handle With Care—Scientists in Industry Often Baffle the Bosses:"

Listen to the tale of a tardy physicist. A brilliant scientist, he was hired by a big Eastern research laboratory after many years in the academic world. Not long after joining the company, he began showing up at his office at 9:30 although the company's working day began at 9 A.M.

The vice president in charge of the physicist's department seethed in silence for several months but at last he approached the scientist with a gentle reminder that 9 A.M. was the customary starting time. The scientist blandly replied that he found the most convenient commuter train to be one which brought him to the office at 9:30 A.M.—and continued to report for work a half hour late.

The incident sounds trivial, and taken alone it is. But the case of the unpunctual physicist points up a major problem puzzling many businessmen today: How do you keep the growing number of top-rank scientists who are moving from college campuses to industrial laboratories happy in their new surroundings?[23]

How indeed? And how do social scientists feel about organization rules and regulations? We shall delve into this aspect in much more detail in the next chapter. At this point, let us see how the social scientists reacted to a statement that was taken from one of the studies of physical scientists in industry:

The professional in industry is expected to accommodate himself to rules and regulations but he often resists and resents them.

	Per cent			
By field of social science	*Agree*	*Disagree*	*Undecided*	*Total*
Economists	81	15	4	100
Psychologists	62	30	8	100
Sociologists	78	22	0	100
Statisticians	76	12	12	100
By organizational level				
Top Management	81	19	0	100
Middle Management	69	21	10	100
Bottom Management	71	23	6	100
By type organization				
Manufacturing	71	27	2	100
Finance	77	9	14	100
Service	74	17	9	100
Public Utility	60	40	0	100
Research laboratory	83	6	11	100

The high amount of agreement with the above statement by all social scientists, regardless of position in the organization or type of company, is especially noteworthy. The very few who were undecided shows that the depth of feeling on this question is pronounced. Additional insights are provided by the write-in comments:

The manager of the planning department of a large oil company agreed with the statement but added: "If he resists or resents rules and regulations, he would be a wise man to understand that he will be more effective if he does accommodate himself to them."

The vice-president of research for an advertising agency commented: "The statement is true but the real question is whether that resentment is justified or not."

The department head of a statistics group at a chemical products company agreed and added: "Some physical restrictions typical of factory operation still prevail in scientific groups and do cause considerable concern, but some of these rules are necessary and should be understood in that light."

The manager of research development at an advertising agency agreed with the statement but pointed out that "when it comes to petty rules or regulations, the scientist can 'get away with murder' if he knows how full or empty the reservoir of management good will toward him is at any time."

A member of the technical staff at a communications research laboratory said, "There is little genuine resistance or resentment to rules and regulations because we don't have many. Have you noticed how people are dressed around here? Pretty informal, wouldn't you say? Come back during the summer and you'll really see some characters, especially those Bermuda short wearers."

The write-in comments together with the data in the last table point up a real problem for administrative-minded managers. It is difficult for a large company, especially at the corporate headquarters where most social scientists work, to allow people to come and go as they please. Top executives are frequently the first to arrive in the morning and the last to leave at night. Sometimes this occurs because they want to "set a good example." More often, it is because they are overworked and want to have some time free from the pressure of telephone calls and meetings. In multi-plant corporations, the executives are fully aware of the fact that they are being constantly observed in their comings and goings by people in the operating companies when they visit headquarters. They know that actions speak louder than words in this area of administration.

SUMMARY OF FINDINGS

In this chapter we have seen how social scientists in industry react to various aspects of their work, and have compared their feelings with their colleagues' in the physical sciences. Disagreements as well as agreements have been noted between the two kinds of scientists. These findings lead us to an inescapable conclusion: sweeping generalities about "scientists in industry" are suspect for two major reasons: (1) Most studies have not separated the reactions of Ph.D.s from those of non-Ph.D.s and (2), Most studies have been carried out with physical scientists at research laboratories often far removed from corporate headquarters. As has been repeatedly mentioned, social scientists in industry are mainly to be found in close contact with top management in their companies. This is hardly ever true of "bench" physical scientists in research laboratories.

Areas of Agreement

Some of the findings about physical scientists do apply to social scientists, as we have seen, but often in ways that are markedly different from those portrayed by some writers about "scientists in industry." The outstanding example is that involving autonomy. Our comparison with the Pelz-Andrews study showed that two-thirds of the scientists with Ph.D. degrees felt that they enjoyed substantial autonomy in their work. Pelz had previously observed in a petrochemical laboratory that the company had been successful in building strong motivation among its professional people by giving them a large measure of individual responsibility. The process was referred to as "controlled freedom." A general problem was sketched out for the scientist; he was shown what mountain to climb and then it was up to him to get to the top. But he was not ignored. He met periodically with other people to whom his work was important such as R. & D. directors, customers, or manufacturers. These meetings kept the research man on his toes, funneled useful information to him and, in particular, gave his upper level executives a chance to appreciate his work.[24]

Physical scientists and social scientists were about equal in favorable reactions about communicating important ideas to those in management who needed to know or who should be interested in what the scientists had to say. Only the statisticians had some difficulty in this area.

As for rules and regulations, there is no question that all scientists dislike them and only tolerate the organization's administrative requirements. As we shall see in the next chapter, this is one of the causes of dissatisfaction of social scientists in industry.

Finally, and perhaps most importantly since so many writers have emphasized the point, there is considerable doubt that Ph.D. scientists in industry have major concern about how they appear in the eyes of their professional colleagues outside their own organizations, especially those in non-industrial settings. This study, and the Pelz-Andrews data, do not support such a contention.

Areas of Disagreement

Physical scientists in industry do not regard the opinions of top executives in their organization as being important for their work. This feeling is in marked contrast to the attitudes of social scientists, especially economists and sociologists. The basic cause can be attributed to the nature of their work. Physical scientists, whether in basic or applied research, do not worry very much about finding commercial applications of their work. It is a wise management that allows such highly trained people plenty of time and freedom to pursue what interests them but at the same time provides the scientists with problems that need solutions. The key figures in research laboratories are not the top executives of the company but the supervisors and group leaders in the laboratory. Social scientists, on the other hand, are in constant communication with the decision makers at headquarters, especially on short-run as well as long-run planning. Mutual respect is a natural result as they work together on problems of the organization.

Social scientists do not accept the notion that research projects should be initiated or stopped solely on the decision of the individual scientist. Perhaps their closer proximity to the users of their work and the opportunity for conferences with higher executives, customers, and other departments, is the major reason for this feeling. They are involved in cost analyses, budget planning, and allocation of resources, both physical and human, and are expected to help top management with research and studies to arrive at sound decisions. Some of the decisions logically call for cessation of unproductive research.

Finally, our data show that economists, psychologists, and sociologists are more highly involved in their work than are physical scientists and statisticians. This was true in all types of organizations except research laboratories. This finding does not square with some of the current writings about scientists in industry.

The sum total of agreements and disagreements between social scientists and physical scientists in industry is not large; there are many more similarities than dissimilarities *when comparisons of attitudes are made between scientists with doctoral degrees.*

In the next chapter we shall be probing in greater depth the reactions of the respondents to aspects of their work, as we look for the causes of satisfactions and dissatisfactions among highly trained social scientists in industry.

SATISFACTIONS AND DISSATIS-
FACTIONS OF SOCIAL SCIENTISTS
IN INDUSTRY

6

In this chapter we shall be delving, in some depth, into the causes of satisfactions and dissatisfactions of the respondents. Hopefully, we shall gain more insight on the motivational forces at work in corporations and their research laboratories where social scientists are employed full-time. Eli Ginzberg and John Herma sounded a warning, based on their research study of talented people, that isolated statements that people make about their work seldom, if ever, represent their feelings about the entirety of their positions in organization life, or in their professional lives. They frequently make both positive and negative statements about their jobs.[1]

In the many attitude surveys carried out by industrial companies intended to reveal the feelings of their employees toward the company, its management, supervision, and a host of other aspects of the work situation, it had always been assumed that there was a direct correlation between high morale and high productivity and its obverse, low morale and low productivity. Arthur Brayfield and William Crockett shattered this illusion. They could not find a single published study among many that asserted such a connection that showed a morale-productivity relationship.[2] Other researchers have raised the same doubts and have documented their findings, from which they determined that "morale," however determined, was only one factor to be considered when attempting to get at the causes of high or low productivity.[3]

We shall begin by examining the responses of the industrial social scientists and comparing them with those of the physical scientists in industry to see whether there are significant differences, and whether such measures provide possible clues to assist in the development of a realistic approach to the administrative problems of highly trained people.

PRODUCTIVITY MEASURES FOR SCIENTISTS

Q. Over the past five years, about how many of the following have you had?

Mean Number for Those Who Replied

	Physical Scientists	Economists	Psychologists	Sociologists	Statisticians
Patents or copyrights	1.69	.17	.28	.06	.10
Published papers	2.31	2.93	2.57	3.95	4.52
Published books	.08	.32	.04	.33	.20
Unpublished reports inside or outside of present organization	8.23	11.2	24.5	12.2	16.1

The only figures above that seem to offer possible productivity measures for social scientists in industry are those that reflect output of published papers and unpublished reports. The latter, obviously, are of greatest value to the organization; whereas the former provide additional ego satisfaction, especially for those who are concerned about their professional reputations outside of their organizations. As we have already noted, this aspect is not of prime importance to Ph.D. scientists in industry.

During the interviews, inquiries were made to get a "feel" of the importance of publication of papers for social scientists in private enterprise. One question was worded somewhat in this manner: "Do you think it is important for your career in this company to write papers for publication in professional journals or to present such papers at professional meetings?" The replies were quite varied; there was no single theme expressed. Some of the respondents, especially former academicians, felt that they did more writing than when they were teachers in colleges or universities and pointed out that this aspect was an important part of their work even though papers and reports were rarely published. The general response was that most companies were reluctant to see such reports published; it wasn't worth the time and effort on the part of the professionals to "clear" them for publication through administrative channels.

Some of the respondents quite candidly admitted that their companies encouraged publication of papers, especially when presented at professional meetings, so that they could be used as "window dressing" for prospective clients or customers. Such expressions came mainly from social scientists employed in companies that submitted proposals for government contracts.

Social scientists were often pressed by management to prepare research reports quickly so that they could be used internally or externally to meet deadlines. As we shall see later in this chapter, this aspect was a pervasive source of discontent for the respondents.

Herbert Shepard has pointed out that rewarding scientific people in industry for good performance presents a difficult administrative problem. "In American industrial society," he wrote, "success is measured largely by the size of the organization one controls. Scientists and engineers are themselves somewhat ambivalent about organizational advancement. On the one hand, it may be regarded as the only generally accepted evidence of their value. On the other hand, they fear loss of professional status and competence. Even laboratory officials who have been many years away from the bench are likely to 'keep their hand in' by working on some technical project. While this indulgence may be to some extent sentimental, it is also a means of preserving professional self-respect."[4]

CAUSES OF SATISFACTIONS AND DISSATISFACTIONS

We shall return to the subject of performance and rewards for scientific personnel in the next chapter, when we shall be listening to the responses of social scientists to questions concerning their career aspirations. At this point in our study let us see whether we can obtain some insight into the causes of satisfactions and dissatisfactions of highly trained people working in industry.

Q. On balance, do you feel that in terms of your earlier expectations your present work provides the satisfactions and rewards you had expected by this time?

	Per cent			
	Econo- mists	Psychol- ogists	Sociol- ogists	Statis- ticians
Yes	82	74	83	70
No	17	21	17	30
N.A.*	1	1	0	0
	100	100	100	100

*N.A. is used to denote no answer or written replies such as "nothing," "can't think of any," "none," and the like.

In gross terms it seems quite apparent that, by and large, most of the social scientists had achieved or saw favorable prospects for achieving their personal goals at the time they started their careers in industry. The fact that very few avoided the question is significant for our analysis: Feelings were apparently quite marked one way or the other.

How does level in the organization affect responses to the same question? Can we assume that the greatest affirmation would be in top management, the least in bottom management, and those in middle management somewhere in between? Such an assumption would seem logical. Let us see from the next table.

**Satisfactions and Rewards in Terms of Earlier Expectations and
Level in the Organization**

	Per cent		
	Top Management	Middle Management	Bottom Management
Yes	80	90	64
No	20	9	30
N.A.	0	1	6
	100	100	100

The responses to the question when broken out in relation to level in the organization were somewhat unexpected. The fact that one in five of the top managers did not have an affirmative feeling about having met earlier expectations adds importantly to our understanding of motivation for people in high positions in industry, especially professionals. We certainly cannot assume that all is well in the upper stratum of an organization. On the other hand, the revelation that middle managers were more satisfied than their hierarchical superiors might have been expected. They do have greater opportunities for keeping their hands in research projects, are less subject to administrative chores, and look forward to new and challenging problems for which their superiors have already "done battle" before they were approved.

The responses of those in bottom management were also about what we might have expected. Yet, almost two-thirds of them expressed satisfaction. However, it should not be comforting for top management to learn that a third of its high-talent professionals, so difficult to recruit in the first place, were not fully satisfied with their career hopes.

Finally, in the area of expectations, we should know what effect, if any, resulted from the type of organization in which the professional social scientists worked:

Satisfactions and Rewards in Terms of Earlier Expectations and Type of Organization

	Per cent			
	Yes	*No*	*N.A.*	*Total*
Public Utility	90	10	0	100
Service	87	13	0	100
Manufacturing	75	23	2	100
Finance	74	13	13	100
Research Lab.	72	28	0	100

The over-all picture shows that, regardless of type of science, level in the organization, or kind of enterprise, a large majority of the social scientists indicated that their earlier expectations in present work provided the satisfactions and rewards that they had expected at this stage of their careers in industry.

We saw in an earlier chapter that social scientists were attracted to positions in industry on a full-time basis for a number of intrinsic and extrinsic reasons. The preliminary data have indicated that the expectations of a large majority of the respondents had been satisfied. The word "satisfaction," however, is somewhat elusive. It should be of greater interest to the reader to know in more detail what the respondents had in mind when they gave affirmative replies to the question posed about satisfying earlier expectations at the time of joining the organization. One way to dig deeper into attitudes is to ask another question that will bring into sharper focus what we are trying to observe. Accordingly, a second question was asked: "What aspects of work *exceeded* earliest expectations?" Put in another way, we could say to the respondents: "All right, you have said that, by and large, your first hopes for a satisfying career were met. What aspects of your *present* work have *exceeded* those first hopes?" The next three tables show their responses in percentage terms. Since the individuals could indicate more than one area of satisfaction, the columns will add up to more than 100 per cent.

Q. What aspects of your work exceed earlier expectations?

	Per cent			
	Econo-mists	Psychol-ogists	Sociol-ogists	Statis-ticians
EXTRINSIC ASPECTS:				
Salary	17	22	29	21
Position in management	21	11	10	0
INTRINSIC ASPECTS:				
Participation in decision making	31	12	15	11
Variety and interesting problems	6	10	20	5
Autonomy	13	12	10	26
Challenging problems	8	8	0	16
Caliber of superiors	0	6	0	5
Caliber of associates	0	0	0	5
N. A. ("nothing" or no written response)	15	26	19	26

These data can be interpreted in several ways; the zero or low percentages could mean "just about what I expected," giving no clue as to whether this reaction is negative, positive, or of no particular importance. Another is to look at the opposite side of the question, that is, what aspects failed to meet expectations. This we shall do very soon. A third way is to analyze the responses by level in the organization to see whether there are disproportionate results when responses by levels are compared. Finally, we can sort out the responses by types of organizations for the same reason. In the following pages, there will be further breakdowns of responses, by managerial level and kinds of enterprises; and this format will be followed for the remaining questions in this chapter. Let us proceed, then, to examine the data by responses according to position level:

Expectations Exceeded and Level in the Organization

	Per cent		
	Top Management	*Middle Management*	*Bottom Management*
EXTRINSIC ASPECTS:			
Salary	27	44	20
Position in management	25	18	5
INTRINSIC ASPECTS:			
Participation in decision making	27	12	8
Variety and interesting problems	3	5	15
Autonomy	8	4	19
Challenging problems	11	8	3
Caliber of superiors	0	0	6
Caliber of associates	0	0	2
N. A. ("nothing," or no written response)	19	16	26

The outstanding statistic in the above array seems to say that almost half of the middle managers are perhaps receiving more salary than they had originally thought possible in an industrial job for a social scientist, whereas a smaller number in top and bottom staff positions have this feeling.

We still need additional information before attempting an analysis of satisfactions, and so we turn now to the variable of different types of organizations. What effect did this have on the responses?

Again we find one statistic that stands out—those in advertising agencies, consulting companies, opinion research organizations, and others in the service sector say that they are very well paid. Another percentage figure showing that almost half of the statisticians did not have any reason to feel that earlier expectations were exceeded, can perhaps best be understood by the fact that they are youngest in age, are relatively less well paid than

Expectations Exceeded and Type of Organization

	Per cent				
	Manufac-turing	Service	Finance	Public Utility	Research Lab.
EXTRINSIC ASPECTS:					
Salary	16	48	15	23	11
Position in management	18	17	0	15	5
INTRINSIC ASPECTS:					
Participation in decision making	24	8	20	23	11
Variety and interesting problems	8	17	5	8	11
Autonomy	12	8	20	23	11
Challenging problems	8	8	15	8	0
Caliber of superiors	3	0	0	8	5
Caliber of associates	0	0	0	0	5
N. A. ("nothing" or no written response)	21	21	10	15	42

those in the other sciences, and occupy the lowest rungs in staff management at present.

As was done with previous statistical data about aspects of organization life for social scientists in industry, deeper understanding was provided by the write-in comments to various questions. At this point, then, let us hear from some of the respondents the details, in written form, why they felt that earlier expectations had not only been realized, but exceeded.

WRITE-IN COMMENTS

The respondents all made comments in the space provided for this purpose in the questionnaire. Most of the responses were rather terse, but some are worthy of mention because they reflect in descriptive detail more information than can be obtained by quantitive means.

The chief economist of a large bank, holding the rank of vice-president, commented that his experience convinced him that economic theories could be put into practice in his organization. The research director of a fund management company felt that his position gave him the opportunity to link economic and investment research, "a combination that, in my opinion, is not sufficiently used today," he added. A staff economist in an electric products manufacturing company was pleased because, as he wrote, "I have full freedom to analyze and complete assignments in a manner that I consider best."

An industrial psychologist in the top management of a publishing company wrote that he had learned more about his profession than he had anticipated because of his work. The research director of an advertising agency commented that his work not only was very interesting, but exceeded his earlier expectations because "it has potential for giving meaning to my life in terms of what I might contribute." Another industrial psychologist in a large oil company did not expect the amount of important interaction with top management that he experienced in his work; he was very pleased by this aspect of organization life. A staff psychologist in an electronics company wrote: "My salary and other such items were about what I expected, but I was not prepared for the acceptance of concepts and methods of social science that I have found here."

A sociologist, who is in top staff management of a consumer products manufacturing company, wrote: "Remuneration! But, in addition, I have considerable freedom for developing research in areas that I think need doing." A department head in an organization producing rubber products, a sociologist by training, was especially pleased by the pace and scope of problems on which he was asked to undertake research to assist top management before decisions were made. A staff sociologist at a communications research laboratory gained satisfaction from the many research opportunities he saw in the organization and the resources that were made available to him when he undertook studies which were in his field of competence.

A middle management statistician in an aerospace company

had somewhat the same comment: "There are unlimited fields of research that need to be done, and I have the freedom to do those that I think are important." Another statistician who is a member of the technical staff in a research laboratory in a communications company had not anticipated "the extent to which, in a consulting situation, I could be useful to a variety of colleagues in other scientific fields in our organization."

These samples of positive comments, if not accompanied by additional information as to disappointments that were also expressed, could give a one-sided portrayal of the total picture of social scientists in private enterprise. We need, therefore, to look at the other side of earlier expectations. What were some of the areas that were found wanting? Accordingly, another question was asked to bring out the negative aspects. The columns add up to more than 100 per cent because more than one response was received from each of those who replied to the question.

Q. What aspects of your work fell short of expectations?

	Per cent			
	Econo-mists	Psychol-ogists	Sociol-ogists	Statis-ticians
EXTRINSIC ASPECTS:				
Salary	2	4	0	16
Position in management	0	0	0	2
INTRINSIC ASPECTS:				
Lack of challenge and growth	10	28	43	32
Resistance of higher management to new ideas	16	8	15	10
Hard to keep up professionally	12	4	10	26
Caliber of superiors	6	8	10	26
Caliber of associates	4	4	5	0
Autonomy	0	0	0	5
N. A. ("nothing" or no response)	52	46	33	21

When as many as a third, more or less, of the social scientists —except the economists—indicate disappointment with sufficient challenge or growth in their professional lives, we have before us a statistic that should give higher management cause for concern. The extent to which this aspect results from position in the organization or kind of enterprise are variables that should be looked at in the analysis. The next two tables should help to round out the picture.

Aspects Fell Short of Expectations and Level in the Organization

	Per cent		
	Top Management	*Middle Management*	*Bottom Management*
EXTRINSIC ASPECTS:			
Salary	0	3	8
Position in management	0	0	2
INTRINSIC ASPECTS:			
Lack of challenge and growth	24	16	29
Resistance of higher management to new ideas	5	23	11
Hard to keep up professionally	11	5	14
Caliber of superiors	5	8	9
Caliber of associates	3	0	6
Autonomy	0	3	0
N. A. ("nothing," or no response)	69	46	36

Again we note that lack of challenge and growth stands out as an important source of dissatisfaction. It was somewhat surprising that a quarter of those in top staff positions had this feeling. Another important statistic is the one that tells us that a fourth of those in middle management are unhappy because they feel that higher management resists new ideas that are put forth by professionals who are usually in charge of social science research in their companies. Alvin Zander commented on this aspect of organizational life and pointed out that those who are affected by change, a natural consequence when new ideas are presented, may show resistance behavior for a variety of reasons: "One person feels that he has lost prestige by the change. To another it may mean that he has lost power over an area of influence which he formerly controlled; and to a third it may mean that his friends will think less well of him."[5] Resistance to change is an ever-present phenomenon of organization life.

To round out the statistical picture of causes of dissatisfaction for those whose earlier expectations were not met, we should look at this aspect and its relationship to the type of organization in which the respondents work:

Aspects Fell Short of Expectations and Type of Organization

	Per cent				
	Manufac-turing	Service	Finance	Public Utility	Research Lab.
EXTRINSIC ASPECTS:					
Salary	9	0	0	0	0
Position in management	0	0	2	0	0
INTRINSIC ASPECTS:					
Lack of challenge and growth	22	30	10	8	47
Resistance of higher management to new ideas	16	0	25	8	0
Hard to keep up professionally	9	9	20	8	11
Caliber of superiors	6	5	10	15	11
Caliber of associates	2	0	5	15	5
Autonomy	0	5	0	0	0
N. A. ("nothing," or no response)	43	57	30	61	31

The fact that almost half of the social scientists working in research laboratories expressed disappointment that earlier hopes for a challenging career had not been met is an important clue for research administrators in such settings. A number of written reasons were given by the social scientists who felt keenly enough to supply them in the questionnaire.

WRITE-IN COMMENTS

By Statisticians

A middle-level manager in the statistics department of a chemical products manufacturing company: "The science I represent is new to industry. A large fraction of time is spent in known areas rather than in reaching out for new knowledge through research."

A member of the technical staff in an airframe company's research laboratory: "Lack of support for research in my field by higher management; too much insulation from colleagues in other fields in the lab; ineptness of the lab's management."

A statistician in the research laboratory of a chemical products company complained that he was not given enough time for self-generated research.

A member of the technical staff in a communications research laboratory wrote: "I am not working on the solution of really important problems in this organization."

By Economists

A member of top management in newspaper publishing: "There is lack of opportunity to effect systematic solutions to a number of management problems because of residual traditionalism."

A bank vice-president in charge of economic research wrote: "Scholarly output is low; there is not enough time for new research."

A top staff manager in an investment house commented: "Time to develop publishable professional articles just does not exist; writing a book is practically impossible."

A department head in a fund management company said that there was lack of acceptance by older men in that field in economic and investment research. "They still believe in the 'intuitive genius' approach," he wrote.

A bottom-level staff manager in the economics department of an electric products manufacturing company felt that his organization made too little use of his training in economics; he thought he should be much more involved in policy decisions.

By Psychologists

Vice-president in an opinion research organization: "The problems are somewhat limited in scope."

A middle manager in an insurance company felt that there was not enough understanding of psychological research; hence, encouragement of research projects was scanty in his industry.

A bottom-level manager in the research laboratory of an electronics company wrote: "Some of the research seems trivial. Time pressures do not allow for complete systematic investigations."

A member of the technical staff in a research laboratory of a communications company commented: "The research is too engineering-oriented. The subject matter is not as interesting as many other areas of research."

By Sociologists

A top-level staff manager in a metal products company felt that the intellectual challenges of his industry did not equal those found in an academic environment.

A middle manager in an oil company wrote: "There is no personal identification with specific research projects. I have almost no control over the decisions that are made that should take my research into account."

A middle management staff member in a rubber products company commented, "Even the corporation fails to assume responsibility for determining objectives without which research suffers from lack of direction and commitment."

A bottom-level manager in an automobile company felt that there was lack of understanding of what social science research had to offer; hence, receptivity for such research by higher management was also lacking.

MEASURES OF GRATIFICATION IN THE WORK OF SOCIAL SCIENTISTS

At this point in our study, we have seen how the respondents now feel about their careers in industry when measured against their earliest hopes and expectations. It is quite clear that, despite some disappointments, a very large majority feel that their present work does provide the satisfactions and rewards they had expected by this time. We shall sum up at the end of this chapter, but before doing so, additional insight may be provided by asking a final question designed to pinpoint the sources of gratification in their work in industry and, contrariwise, the reasons for lack of gratification. The schema will be similar to that used with expectations.

Q. What do you consider to be the most gratifying aspects of your work?

	Per cent			
	Econo-mists	Psychol-ogists	Sociol-ogists	Statis-ticians
EXTRINSIC ASPECTS:				
Salary	10	10	19	0
Position in management	14	2	0	0
INTRINSIC ASPECTS:				
Professional achievement	58	80	71	42
Participation in decision making	18	18	29	5
Autonomy	22	10	29	31
Variety of problems	2	22	4	21
Attitude of superiors	12	16	5	5
Challenging problems	6	6	5	16
N. A. ("nothing," or no response)	20	17	6	19

NOTE: Columns add up to more than 100 per cent, since respondents could and did give more than one reason.

These data are very revealing of the feelings of social scientists at work full-time in industry. Except for statisticians, well over half of them are gratified by professional achievement. What we do not know is how these data may be affected by two important variables: position in the organization and type of enterprise in which the social scientist is working. The next two tables supply the information:

Level in the Organization and Most Gratfying Aspects

	Per cent		
	Top Management	Middle Management	Bottom Management
EXTRINSIC ASPECTS:			
Salary	16	13	5
Position in management	16	6	0
INTRINSIC ASPECTS:			
Professional achievement	65	72	62
Participation in decision making	40	41	6
Autonomy	16	16	24
Variety of problems	14	13	21
Attitude of superiors	8	11	14
Challenge	8	3	9
N. A. ("nothing," or no response)	5	23	20

Type of Organization and Most Gratifying Aspects

	Per cent				
	Manufac- turing	Service	Finance	Public Utility	Research Laboratory
EXTRINSIC ASPECTS:					
Salary	9	13	15	8	5
Position in management	6	4	10	8	0
INTRINSIC ASPECTS:					
Professional achievement	66	65	60	85	58

Type of Organization and Most Gratifying Aspects (*cont.*)

	Per cent				
	Manufac-turing	*Service*	*Finance*	*Public Utility*	*Research Laboratory*
Participation in decision making	33	17	20	31	5
Autonomy	20	17	30	8	21
Variety of problems	16	35	10	8	11
Attitude of superiors	11	13	10	8	13
Challenge	9	9	5	0	5
N. A. ("nothing," or no response)	17	19	16	17	15

No matter which way we examine the data we find one outstanding gratification in present work: professional achievement. All other aspects pale in significance when measured against this single gratification. The skeptical reader can exclaim, "They are deluding themselves! You have already indicated that the respondents feel that they are the best judges of their own work; that they do not have their work examined critically by members of their own profession outside the organization. Your social scientists also look inside the company for approval of their work. Since the "insiders," by and large, do not have the professional training necessary to make real judgments, how can you accept their responses that they are very gratified by professional achievement?" The best "answer" to the skeptics or the cynics is to examine data that show the length of service with present employers of the respondents. If the social scientist did not provide important professional counsel, and assist in making decisions that often turned on the research data provided by the social scientist in his company, it would be most unlikely that he would be retained as a full-time employee or, more importantly, he would not stay in such an organization.

There is another side to the coin of gratification. The data show quite clearly that salary or position in management are not the most important factors in providing satisfaction for highly trained people in industry, even if they receive compensation in excess of what might be expected in non-industrial organizations. Professionals want professional careers. This requirement looms largest in the decision to stay in industry or to leave it, as we shall see in the next chapter. We already know that the decision to accept employment in private enterprise, in the first place, was highly motivated by a desire on the part of the young Ph.D. in social science to have a challenging professional career.

As with other aspects, additional insight is sometimes provided by reading the descriptions of the most gratifying aspects of work as provided by the respondents by their written or spoken comments. Some representative samples were selected for this purpose; they will be grouped by the various social sciences.

WRITE-IN COMMENTS

By Economists

A top-level staff manager in a metal products company: "Freedom to engage in writing and service on governmental and national business committees."

Two bank vice-presidents gave virtually the same replies: that they were highly gratified by developing young people in their departments to do effective economic research. A top-level staff manager in an oil company put it another way: "I highly appreciate the fact that top management leaves it up to me to train the people under me the way I think they should be trained for professional work."

A vice-president in an investment house: "Carrying out complicated financing projects to completion."

Director of personnel research in a manufacturing company: "Gratified by sense of personal accomplishment and acceptance by other members of top management despite my lack of technical background in a chemistry-based product company."

A middle management economist in an oil company wrote

that he was pleased by his salary and the opportunity to direct work on corporate planning that had a direct effect on the company's future.

Another oil company middle manager gave as his reason for gratification: "Having my forecasts turn out right. Of course, if they didn't, it would be disastrous for me."

A bottom-level staff manager in a bank commented, "I can do the kind of empirical research projects that I greatly enjoy, with computers and clerical help readily available."

Another bottom-level manager stated that he had rather wide freedom to study business-related economic problems and was called upon to suggest appropriate action by the company as a result of his interpretation of studies inside or outside the organization.

By Psychologists

Top management industrial psychologist in an engineering company: "Bringing about necessary changes in organization, people, and attitudes of employees." Another top-level staff manager in a food products manufacturing company wrote that he had influence over corporate policy that benefited thousands of employees.

A middle management director of research in an advertising agency was gratified by the knowledge that his work was important to the firm and was also important to society in general.

A middle-level staff manager in a consumer products company wrote: "Satisfaction from meaningful and significant contributions to problem-solving; respect from my superiors because of my unique contributions; good pay and opportunity for more."

An oil company industrial psychologist was pleased because he had many opportunities to influence the organization in ways leading to better utilization of human resources.

A member of the technical staff in the research laboratory of an aerospace company gave as his reasons, "The opportunity to develop new research methods; bringing social science research into an engineering-physical science oriented organization."

An industrial psychologist in an oil company was especially gratified because he was making full use of his knowledge and skills, had colleagues of high technical competence, congenial co-workers, and opportunities to work on problems of central importance to the company.

A member of the technical staff of a communications company research laboratory wrote: "Freedom to select and define problems; use of my work by others."

By Sociologists

A top management staff member in an insurance company: "Freedom to allocate my own time; the excitement of creating a new role in a business organization."

Vice-president of a consumer opinion research company: "Independence; opportunity to pursue professional interests; variety of problems."

A top management sociologist of a metal products company was gratified by "complete freedom to work on behalf of the employees of this business organization and ready access to the president of the company to hear my ideas."

The director of research in an advertising agency wrote: "The intellectual challenge, the opportunities for constant diversity in types of problems; the financial rewards."

A rubber products manufacturing company middle manager was particularly pleased by his feeling of contribution to international, economic, and social integration and development."

A bottom-level staff manager in a communications company: "Chance to be influential in introducing social science findings into practical situations."

Another bottom-level staff manager, this one in an automobile company, was gratified by the variety of problems and the fact that his work had to meet very high professional standards to be accepted.

By Statisticians

A middle manager in a chemical products company: "Bringing along younger people in my profession by teaching them how to tackle unstructured problems."

A consumer products company middle manager wrote: "The recognition that mathematics and statistics are making important contributions to the company's success."

An airframe company statistician: "My theoretical results and their experimental confirmation."

A member of the technical staff in the research laboratory of a business machine and electronics company felt that he was working to develop knowledge that would improve the living standards of mankind.

A bottom-level manager in the research laboratory of a chemical products company was gratified by the amount of autonomy he had in directing the people under him in solving problems.

SOURCES OF DISSATISFACTION

At the start of this chapter, it was pointed out that when people are asked about their work, they often give both positive and negative responses about their roles in the organization. As we have already seen, the respondents did not hesitate to indicate their displeasure with some aspects of their work. It was to be expected that they would not be entirely gratified by their work in industry. To complete our survey of attitudes we should, therefore, be informed about those aspects that were least gratifying to the social scientists in their industrial careers. The next three tables, followed by write-in comments, will give us this kind of information.

Q. What do you consider to be the least gratifying aspects of your work?

	Per cent			
	Econo- mists	Psychol- ogists	Sociol- ogists	Statis- ticians
EXTRINSIC ASPECTS:				
Administrative details, paper work, budgets, etc.	30	24	33	26
Hours	12	8	10	5
Salary	0	4	5	5
INTRINSIC ASPECTS:				
Resistance to new ideas by superiors and others	25	28	29	16
Attitude toward research by supe- riors and associates	14	20	29	16
Pressure for quick results	6	5	5	0
Not enough involve- ment in the decision making processes	6	12	5	32
No opportunity to publish or attend professional meetings	6	3	5	0
Incompetent subordinates	4	2	0	10
N. A. ("nothing," or no response)	27	18	22	24

NOTE: Columns add up to more than 100 per cent since respondents could and did give more than one reason.

Least Gratifying Aspects and Level in the Organization

	Per cent		
	Top Management	*Middle Management*	*Bottom Management*
EXTRINSIC ASPECTS:			
Administrative details, paper work, budgets, etc.	33	29	24
Hours	16	5	8
Salary	3	3	3
INTRINSIC ASPECTS:			
Resistance to new ideas by superiors and others	19	26	27
Attitude toward research by superiors and associates	16	13	21
No opportunity to publish or attend professional meetings	14	0	3
Pressure for quick results	7	2	6
Incompetent subordinates	6	5	2
Not enough involvement in the decision making processes	0	5	21
N. A. ("nothing," or no response)	21	27	25

Least Gratifying Aspects and Type of Organization

	Per cent				
	Manufac- turing	Service	Finance	Public Utility	Research Laboratory
EXTRINSIC ASPECTS:					
Administrative de- tails, paper work, budgets, etc.	31	22	25	33	26
Hours	12	9	20	23	16
Salary	8	0	0	0	4
INTRINSIC ASPECTS:					
Resistance to new ideas by superiors and associates	34	9	20	23	30
Attitude toward re- search by supe- riors and associates	15	9	20	23	30
Not enough involve- ment in the de- cision making processes	9	13	15	8	16
No opportunity to publish or attend professional meetings	8	0	7	0	0
Pressure for quick results	4	9	4	0	4
Incompetent subordinates	2	5	5	8	5
N. A. ("nothing," or no response)	18	23	23	25	25

We now have before us some statistical information that is not difficult to analyze. It is obvious that a fair number of the respondents—about a third—dislike administrative detail with its concomitant paper work as well as having to deal with personnel problems, preparation of budgets, and other bureaucratic chores. This is not an unexpected finding—one that plagues scientifically oriented management more, perhaps, than others in the organization. The statistics are consistent in that it made little difference when related to type of science, level in the organization, or type of enterprise; this aspect was an important source of dissatisfaction. Some descriptive details will be seen in the written comments to follow.

Another significant source of dissatisfaction comes from the tensions caused by the resistance of hierarchical superiors and associates to new ideas that are proposed by social scientists— primarily the kind of behavior that indicates resistance to change.

The third major source of restiveness, closely allied to the one just mentioned, is the attitude of some higher managers and peers who, in the opinion of the social scientists, do not show the same respect for the "soft" sciences as they do for the "hard" sciences. This was especially noteworthy in research laboratories where physical scientists are dominant.

It was to be expected that those in bottom management, especially statisticians, were unhappy because they were not involved enough in the decision making processes.

The pressure in academia to "publish or perish" does not develop in private enterprise. Companies encourage their highly trained people to attend professional meetings; annual dues in professional associations are usually paid, as are travel expenses to meetings, especially when papers are presented. The lack of attendance at such meetings or the paucity of papers presented by industrial social scientists does not necessarily mean opposition on the part of the organization. On the contrary, many companies have a self-interest in making it possible for highly trained people to keep up professionally. As to publication of papers, this aspect does present a dilemma for the company. It does not want its competitors to profit from research that it has undertaken, often at great expense. At the same time, there is recognition of the professional's need for ego-satisfaction in order to hold him. As is so often the case in human affairs, compromises are worked out that are not always satisfactory. A statistical reading of dissatisfaction, as revealed in the last three tables, does not seem to indicate that the lack of opportunity to publish papers or to attend professional meetings is of major significance.

To complete our fund of information on the sources of dissatisfaction for social scientists in industry, we turn now to the descriptions offered by the written comments that were added to the negative replies when the respondents were asked about aspects of their work that were least gratifying.

WRITE-IN COMMENTS

By Economists

A top management staff member in an oil company: "Long hours and having to re-do so much of the work of my staff to have it meet the standards I want my department to uphold."

The head of the economics department of a metal products manufacturer complained of the necessity to continuously "resell" the importance of economic analysis in his company because of the large number of changes in management personnel. A similar comment was made by a middle management staff member of a business machine company who added: "Starting from scratch and explaining concepts every time a change needs to be made."

The vice-president of an investment house wrote, "Dealing with local political environments on municipal bond issues is sometimes very frustrating."

Director of research for a newspaper publisher: "Obstructionism and status quo attitudes of key executives." A similar complaint was lodged by a middle management economist in an automobile company when he commented that he had difficulty persuading other people in the organization to accept and act on the implementation of research findings that were contrary to established concepts.

A bottom management respondent, who is employed in an electronics manufacturing company, stated that he was unhappy about "the unbalanced work load, the uneven flow of significant assignments, and top management inattention to reports and recommendations followed by periods of crisis action."

The major cause for negative feelings—administrative chores —was described in a variety of ways:

Necessity to do trivial work that is inevitably part of the over-all job.
There are some routine aspects I would love to get rid of. I don't like routine work at all.
Useless paper work; reporting systems.
Administrative details such as departmental budgeting and expense account approval.
Unavoidable trivia.

A complaint often heard in professional circles, regardless of the field, was succinctly stated by a middle manager in a management consultant company: "Limitations of delegation of work because of the small size of our group which, for me, means doing a lot of low-level work such as library search, statistical computations, proof-reading of reports, and the like, that could be more efficiently done by junior men or graduate students."

By Psychologists

Vice-president of an advertising agency: "The professional aspects; I don't do the research myself."

Director of research in another advertising agency: "I must avoid looking too much like an impractical egghead to superiors, associates, and clients while simultaneously struggling to get out from under the 'huckster' labels pinned on me by professionals outside the industry."

A director of personnel research for an insurance company was not happy because of the "on-again-off-again" attitudes toward research in his company.

An oil company industrial psychologist: "The hack work— time consuming attention to details of no consequence."

Two psychologists in research laboratories added comments, the first from a business machine company's research center: "Routine aspects; middle management inertia; the penny-wise-pound-foolish attitudes toward our kind of research." The other, in an aerospace company wrote: "The lack of understanding of social science disciplines displayed by certain management personnel and co-workers makes it hard to contribute fully."

A member of the personnel staff in a steel manufacturing company said that his management failed to use the best information available, including his work, to solve organization problems. As a result, he often found himself working on problems that he did not think were of real importance for the company.

A member of the technical staff at an airframe company's research facility added to his notation why he was less than gratified by all aspects of his work: "Hours of work and rigid attitudes toward them; time continuity in research studies not understood by management."

An industrial psychologist for an oil company wrote: "Day-to-day interruption of one's longer range (ostensibly useful) work. 'Putting out fires' that would go out by themselves if we could apply a little more 'tincture of neglect.' "

A physiological psychologist in a pharmaceutical company's research laboratory felt that there were too many compromises with superiors, poor work facilities—no private office, and a forty-hour nine-to-five kind of job that he believed was inefficient for the kinds of research problems in which he was involved.

The last three comments were voiced in various ways by quite a few of the respondents trained in psychology. A number of top and middle management staff people complained about the paper-work routine and what some termed "administrative trivia."

By Sociologists

A top-level staff manager in a communications research company: "Red tape; accounting; budgets."

A vice-president in a consumer products research organization: "Routine chores; terrible overworking; lack of intrinsic interest in many of the problems; lack of common interests with many business clients."

A middle manager in an oil company was dissatisfied by "bureaucratic delay and unwillingness of management to 'take a chance.' "

A sociologist who is in middle management in a rubber products company felt that there was corporate disorganization with respect to purpose, objectives, policies, and structural relations, all of which contributed to wasted effort for accomplishing what needed to be done in his field to be of value to the company.

A member of the technical staff of a communication company research laboratory commented: "Working with engineers who fail to have the kind of understanding I think they should have about social science research."

A bottom-level management man in an electronics and communications company wrote: "There are lots of dumb people in very high jobs. One wonders, 'How come?' Sheer rank gives them far more power than rank does in a university." This comment stirred up a sardonic response to academicians that had appeared in a paper read by an industrial socciologist at the 1962 annual meeting of the American Sociological Association:

A recent issue of *The Listener* reports a conversation between two professors as they left a conference of business men. The one remarked, "I can't quite understand how business men manage to be so successful in life when they obviously have such limited talent." "But my dear chap," said the other professor, "it's really quite simple. They only have other business men to compete with."[6]

Carlson's story, apocryphal or not, applies to many of the scattered comments made by several respondents in every one of the social sciences. Their attitudes toward higher management, non-social science colleagues or associates, clients, and customers, has already been reflected in the last three tables under the headings "Resistance to new ideas by superiors and associates" and "Attitude toward research by superiors and associates." The percentage figures, as we have already noted, are high enough to warrant further exploration of these causes by companies that employ social scientists—and other scientists —full time.

Sociologists were also annoyed by administrative chores; as many as a third registered this feeling, including a number who are in vice-presidential and other top management posts.

By Statisticians

A middle manager in an aerospace manufacturing company: "Dealing with personality problems; other administrative jobs that I must, of necessity, deal with."

Another middle management staff member in a consumer products manufacturing company: "The failure to convince advertising people that we can be of use to them."

An insurance company middle manager: "Working with men of little vision."

A member of the technical staff in an airframe company's research facility: "The low repute, both in the community and the profession, that my company holds. The viciousness and pettiness of the laboratory management. The lack of recognition."

Three write-in comments speak for themselves. The first was from a statistician employed in the research facility of a business machine company: "My capability is not being fully used." The next came from a staff member of the statistics group in a consumer products company: "I am not fully rewarded financially for the importance of my work." Finally, this one was contributed by a member of the technical staff of a communications research laboratory: "I don't like the business of accounting for my time on forms."

SUMMARY

1. A large majority of social scientists, not less than 7 out of 10, feel that in terms of rewards and satisfactions they had expected when they accepted employment in private industry,

their earlier expectations had been met. This feeling was reflected by most respondents and was somewhat affected by position in management or type of company in which the scientist worked.

When asked what aspects of their work exceeded earlier expectations, about a quarter of the respondents selected salary. Those in middle management were especially pleased with their compensation. In the service-type companies, salary was mentioned by almost half of the respondents as an expectation that had been exceeded.

Another important source of satisfaction, especially indicated by economists, was their involvement in the decision making processes in their organizations.

2. There were some aspects of work that did not satisfy earlier expectations; the most important lack was expressed by sociologists when they indicated that their present work did not provide enough professional challenge and growth. A third of the statisticians had this feeling, as did a quarter of the psychologists. Only a few economists displayed lack of satisfaction with this aspect of their work.

When viewed in relation to position in management, it was surprising to find that a quarter of those in top management registered dissatisfaction with lack of challenge and professional growth. Those in advertising agencies, opinion research companies, and management consulting firms were noticeably not satisfied in this respect.

Another aspect that was not appreciated, especially by social scientists in middle management positions in financial types of organizations such as banks and investment companies, was resistance of higher management to new ideas suggested as a result of social science research findings.

3. When asked what aspects of their work were most gratifying, the outstanding response was a feeling of professional achievement through their work in industry. This was true of all social scientists to a very high degree, and especially felt by psychologists, sociologists, those in middle management posi-

tions, and by social scientists employed in public utility companies.

An important source of gratification, but not to the same degree as professional achievement, was their involvement in the decision making processes in their organizations, in particular for the respondents in top and middle management position in their companies. In service companies, lack of professional challenge and growth was offset to some degree by the variety of problems encountered in their work.

4. The major source of lack of gratification stemmed from a general dislike with the administrative aspects of the work of industrial social scientists. They were irritated by forms, budgets, dealing with personnel problems, and other types of work that involved red tape and paper work. This was true in all types of companies and at every level in staff management.

Gratification with present work was lessened by annoyance with the attitude of some superiors and peers in the organization who resisted new ideas that were presented to them by the social scientists, and by the attitudes of such people toward social science research.

5. Despite assertions by some writers that scientists in industry were greatly displeased by their inabiilty to publish the results of their work in professional journals, or to present such findings at professional meetings, there was surprisingly little indication of such dissatisfaction by social scientists in private enterprise. Curiously enough, the few who did indicate some negative feeling on this aspect were mainly to be found in top positions in staff management in their organizations. Those in bottom management, especially in research laboratories, had indicated in various ways that they were not as generally satisfied with all aspects of their work as was the case with those in higher levels or in other types of organizations. We might have expected that negative feelings would be exacerbated if blocks were put in the way of research laboratory social scientists, or those in lower management, to publish professional articles or deliver papers at meetings of their professional colleagues. Such was not the case with those particular respondents.

CONCLUSION

It is fair to conclude that social scientists in industry are, to a very high degree, satisfied with their work. Their earlier hopes for fruitful professional careers had not only been met, they had been exceeded. Salary levels were especially pleasing, but of greater importance as sources of satisfaction were such aspects as professional achievement and being drawn into the decision making processes in their organizations.

It is obvious from our findings that alongside feelings of gratification, there are also present causes for dissatisfaction that can reduce the psychic satisfactions that all people, especially highly trained professionals, want from their work. Advertising agencies, management consulting firms, and opinion research organizations apparently provide the least amount of challenge and professional growth, although they do offer a variety of interesting problems to cope with. Such companies can only exist if they provide satisfaction for their clients. The opportunities for doing original and untried kinds of research are minimal in the company-client relationship; they are not overabundant in the other companies, even in research laboratories—which is surprising. Locating the sources of lack of professional challenge and growth is extremely important for companies that are eager to attract and hold highly trained professionals in their organizations. More will be said on this in later chapters when we explore the respondents' feelings about the kinds of careers they want for themselves from now on, and why some leave industry.

To continue the exploration for further insights into the world of work of the social scientist in industry, we turn now, in the next chapter, to the kinds of careers they envisage for themselves in the long run in private enterprise.

HOW SOCIAL SCIENTISTS IN INDUSTRY SEE THEIR FUTURE CAREERS

7

In our industrial world, "getting ahead" to most people means promotions to higher positions with more pay, prestige, power, and influence in the organization with outward manifestations of organization "success": A private secretary, a multiwindowed office—usually near the top bosses—drapes on the windows and rugs on the floor, luncheon in the executive dining room, and other privileges so well characterized by the military in the phrase "rank hath its privileges" known to all in the armed forces as "R.H.I.P." Social scientists in industry are not bereft of such privileges.

Authors of novels of the current scene picture the successful corporation head as a hard-boiled, no-nonsense kind of person, with limited education. If he has a college degree, it is usually in engineering. A small amount of research would reveal that a large majority of the leaders of American business are college graduates, many with master's degrees, and some with doctorates —especially in economics. Four of the respondents in this study, all of them economists with Ph.D.'s, are presidents of their companies. The chief executive officer of the Columbia Broadcasting System holds a doctorate in psychology. A well-known business magazine referred to him as a businessman who devotes himself to research as well as organization and explained briefly how he became connected with CBS.

Stanton got into broadcasting by taking a Ph.D. in psychology at Ohio State University. His dissertation on radio's social effects brought him to CBS' attention in 1935. He became head of the research department and did such a brilliant job that he quickly rose in the corporation. By 1946, at the age of 38, he was president. *The New Yorker* wryly remarked that he was "one of the few men to achieve success despite the handicap of a Ph.D."[1]

The inference above is plain: the possessor of a Ph.D. obviously is not cut out to be a corporation president. When this does happen, as in the case of Dr. Stanton and a few others in American corporate life, it is assumed that such "success" comes not because of the Ph.D., but in spite of it. Is it possible that Ph.D.'s in industry are more interested in their fields than they are in "getting ahead" organizationally by climbing the rungs of the ladder to positions of power and influence? Questions were asked of the respondents aimed at bringing out their feelings about what they thought was important for their careers in the future. The first had to do with projecting their preferences for career development in the decade ahead:

Q. Over the next ten years, which of the following is most likely to be profitable to your career development (however you think of it)?

	Per cent			
	Econo-mists	Psychol-ogists	Sociol-ogists	Statis-ticians
Remain in research in present company	25	38	43	26
Less research and more management in present company	50	12	24	5
Move to research in another company	8	10	14	16

	Per cent			
	Econo- mists	Psychol- ogists	Sociol- ogists	Statis- ticians

Move to less research,
  more management,
  in another company
	2	8	5	16

Leave private enterprise	12	22	14	16
Undecided	3	10	0	21
	100	100	100	100
Stay in private enterprise	85	68	86	63
Leave private enterprise	12	22	14	16
Undecided	3	10	0	21
	100	100	100	100
Stay in research	33	48	57	42
Less research, more management	52	20	29	21

We know from data in previous chapters that economists and sociologists hold the highest positions in management among the respondents. Therefore, it should not be surprising that most of the social scientists in these two fields want to stay in private industry, whereas the psychologists and statisticians are somewhat less inclined to do so. Of particular significance is the fact that half of the economists want to move into high managerial positions, whereas a majority of the other social scientists do not aspire to such careers. The fact that over a third of the psychologists and statisticians see themselves either out of industry or undecided whether to continue their careers as industrial social scientists calls for much more development of their feelings as to where they want to work if they leave private enterprise. We shall be probing this sort of question in the next chapter when we find out from social scientists who left industry why they left and for what kinds of activities. For the present, we should see whether level in the organization or type of company in which employed were significant factors in their replies to the question asked about career plans for the next ten years.

Career Plans and Level in the Organization

	Per cent		
	Top Management	Middle Management	Bottom Management
Remain in research in present company	22	27	42
Less research and more management in present company	49	35	10
Move to research in another company	8	11	10
Move to less research, more management, in another company	0	8	9
Leave private enterprise	18	9	21
Undecided	3	10	8
	100	100	100
Stay in private enterprise	79	81	71
Leave private enterprise	18	9	21
Undecided	3	10	8
	100	100	100
Stay in research	30	38	52
Leave research, more management	49	43	19

It is apparent that once having tasted the fruits of life in industry as a professional social scientist, the desire to remain in that setting is very strong at this time of their lives. It was somewhat surprising, however, to find that almost a fifth of those in top management staff positions expected to leave industry in the next ten years. Some of the respondents in top positions now are probably reaching that age when they have to think about mandatory retirement, in most corporations at sixty-five. From previous data we know that about a quarter of the respondents in top management are now fifty or over. In the other two levels, the percentages are lower. We shall soon be making comparisons between the "stayers" and "leavers" in the next chapter, and shall be in a better position to analyze the importance of age as a factor in the ten-year career projections of those now in the highest level of staff management. How many top management social scientists left their positions for activities outside of industry and at what ages will be determined, for example.

As to those in bottom management, it should be expected that social scientists in this category would be in the majority of those who prefer to have a research career at this stage in their professional development.

Let us look now at data that relates to types of organizations and career planning. To what extent does this factor affect the social scientist's outlook for the future? The next table should help us to arrive at some conclusion on this aspect of career thinking of social scientists in industry:

Career Plans and Type of Organization

	Per cent				
	Manufac-turing	Service	Finance	Public Utility	Research Laboratory
Remain in research in present company	19	38	45	54	46
Less research and more management in present company	37	13	35	15	6
Move to research in another company	11	17	15	0	6
Move to less research more management in another company	8	9	0	8	6
Leave private enterprise	16	23	0	23	20
Undecided	9	0	5	0	16
	100	100	100	100	100
Stay in private industry	75	77	95	77	64
Leave private industry	16	23	0	23	20
Undecided	9	0	5	0	16
	100	100	100	100	100
Stay in research	30	55	60	54	52
Leave research, more management	45	22	35	23	12

Very obviously, the respondents' views for the future were affected by the types of organizations in which they now work. Those employed in financial kinds of companies such as banks, insurance companies, and investment houses, not only want to stay in industry, they expect to continue their careers in their present organizations. Another statistic that stands out is the fact that social scienists in manufacturing companies lean more toward general management than research careers. Because we know that the percentage figures showing the size of the group that will leave industry altogether includes people who are not particularly interested in higher managerial posts, except for those in manufacturing, we must agree with Herbert Krugman's assertion that scientists in managerial positions think of themselves as scientists first and managers second.[2]

WHAT SOCIAL SCIENTISTS WOULD LOOK FOR IN A NEW JOB

The lure of a position in another company is constantly dangled before all scientists—at professional meetings, in large advertisements in such widely read papers as the *Wall Street Journal* and the business section of the Sunday *New York Times,* and through executive recruiters sometimes known as "headhunters." The figures in the last three tables indicate that there is not a great deal of interest in either leaving industry or moving over to another company. Nevertheless, offers are made and no doubt considered. When social scientists with Ph.D.'s are sought, what factors do they consider in making up their minds whether the offer is attractive enough for them to give serious consideration to a move? The respondents were asked a question to bring out the weight they would give to different aspects of a new position. The next table will show the weighted average score for each of the 18 items listed derived by assigning the following values:

Slight or none......1
Moderate 2
Considerable 3

Great 4
Utmost 5

Q. Listed below are different kinds of opportunites which a job might afford. If you were to seek a job, how much importance would you personally attach to each of these (disregarding whether or not your present job provides them)?

Opportunity	Weighted Average Score			
	Econo-mists	Psychol-ogists	Sociol-ogists	Statis-ticians
To grow and learn new knowledge and skills	4.17	3.83	4.06	4.00
To work on difficult and challenging problems	4.08	4.09	4.12	4.05
To have freedom to carry out my own ideas	3.95	3.78	3.94	3.89
To work on problems of central importance to the company	3.93	3.55	3.53	3.63
To be evaluated fairly in proportion to what I contribute	3.77	3.72	3.75	3.79
To make full use of my present knowledge and skills	3.75	3.98	4.18	3.68
To earn a good salary	3.47	3.57	3.53	3.47
To work with colleagues of high technical competence	3.38	3.40	3.56	4.00
To have clear objectives toward which I can aim my work	3.38	3.10	3.71	3.68
To associate with top executives in the organization	3.28	2.71	3.13	2.32
To work on problems of value to the nation's well-being	3.25	2.85	3.17	3.05
To advance in administrative authority and status	3.25	2.67	3.06	2.33
To work under superiors of high technical competence	3.17	2.71	3.25	3.37
To have congenial co-workers as colleagues	3.05	2.71	3.25	3.37
To contribute to broad knowledge in my field	3.00	3.04	3.17	3.68
To advance in the professional respect of colleagues	2.93	2.84	3.56	4.00
To build my professional reputation outside this company	2.90	2.76	3.19	3.47
To have stability of employment	2.72	2.79	2.56	3.16

As we examine the data horizontally as well as vertically, it is quite obvious that, except for a few aspects, the rank order of opportunities that might be sought in a new job are just about the same for all social scientists in industry. There are some differences that do stand out. For example, statisticians are least concerned whether or not they associate with top executives in the company but do give considerable weight to working with colleagues of high technical competence and to advancement in the professional respect of their colleagues. Statisticians also have little interest in advancing to higher managerial posts and concomitant status. They do give more weight to stability of employment than any of the other social scientists, all of whom place this item last or close to the bottom in their list of desirable aspects of a new position.

Salary is not unimportant. It is very interesting that this aspect was placed almost equally in the scale for all of the respondents, quite important but ranked below several intrinsic factors. If the reader looks for scores of 4.00 or higher, he will quickly note those opportunities that are held in highest esteem for a fruitful career. Very obviously, opportunities to grow in the respondent's profession, to work on difficult and challenging problems, and to make full use of his long training loom largest in the decision to accept another position in industry if one was offered or if his present job was not providing these desired objectives. As has been stated, salary is certainly an important consideration too, but other factors outweigh this aspect of employment. The lowest paid of the respondents, the statisticians, were much more concerned with having a position that would afford opportunities to work with colleagues of high technical competence, and to be held in professional esteem in the eyes of their colleagues than to increase their earnings.

One of the troublesome problems when making judgments based on scores or percentages is that of giving meaning to numbers. Whenever we try to quantify feelings that are expressed in check marks we are faced with the possibility of misinterpretation, despite the most careful efforts to code such responses for machine tabulation. As John Wilkinson pointed out, anyone who has ever had the experience of programing computing devices has had the distressing feeling of knowing that he has to put aside value judgments to process the information into something quantitative. "There is an inescapable tendency to begin to function as a machine oneself," he wrote.[3] That is why efforts were made to obtain additional information through interviews and the write-in comments.

Two respondents who stayed in private industry but changed jobs provided insight on why some social scientists make such moves in order to carry on fruitful careers. A sociologist who was the manager of human factors and training for a large electronics products corporation for five years explained why he changed jobs:

I was employed by the company to develop a training program relating to the implementation of a to-be-developed mechanized information storage and retrieval system for a government group. This goal was not met because of the cancellation of the contract. However, I remained with the group to head up a Human Factors and Training Group where we supported, through developmental work, proposal writing and contractual work for a larger group concerned with the general area of information systems. My salary was increased from $14,000 to $18,000 in this position. Further improvement in my position came only with my acceptance in the same organization of the job of Manager of Program Engineering. After five years in the company, I was laid off because of a decline in business. After a short stretch with a small research company, I left to take my present position.

This social scientist felt that he had been exploited by the first company because there wasn't a real career opportunity for him. Short-run budget limitations took precedence over the building of a research group for that corporation.

An industrial psychologist, who joined the technical staff of a research laboratory in the communications field when he obtained his Ph.D., spent nine years in that activity before deciding to leave the lab and ask for a transfer to an operating arm of the same corporation. A new world opened up for him as a result of this move (which he intiated), and he explained why:

At the lab I had something of everything: opportunity to explore, to solve people's problems, some status, fairly good pay, and some influence, but I was not really succeeding. I was not a true scientist, a really influential professional, nor an administrator. In my present job I am a big step forward toward being an influential professional in the company.

We know from other studies that highly educated people become frustrated when their capabilities are not fully used. This is true of virtually all human beings, of course, but in the case of scientific and professional employees, feelings on this score are more intense, more easily aroused. This was a major finding from a number of conferences held on the subject of utilization of scientific and professional manpower by the National Manpower Council.[4]

The data in this and other chapters have clearly shown that when there is opportunity to be fully professional, to work in an atmosphere of intellectual understanding and acceptance of the work of social scientists, professionals in industry are highly motivated to continue their careers in organizations that provide the climate for self-actualization. Abraham Maslow described such individuals as people who are able through their own creative abilities to derive great satisfaction from their work. "They are attracted to mystery, to novelty, to change, flux, and find these all easy to live with," he wrote. "These people, the self-actualizing individuals tend, on the contrary, to be easily bored with monotony, with fixity, and with lack of change," he concluded.[5]

CAREERS AND VALUES

"I believe that the goals and values of a scientist and of a business organization are often in conflict and that is a source of a good deal of job dissatisfaction," said an industrial psychologist when interviewed at a research laboratory of a communications company. Pressed to explain what he had in mind, he responded by saying that he felt quite comfortable in his position because he saw his role primarily as one of producing new knowledge. "I know that the company has to make a profit; I'm not against that, but I don't concern myself with how profits are made as long as I am satisfied that my work is professional and useful."

A number of writers have been concerned with sources of discontent of intellectuals in our present-day world. Henry May has pointed out that economic self-assertion still remains to most Americans a sort of moral obligation, while self-fulfillment still looks like a pretty word for selfishness. "Yet self-fulfillment through science, or literature, or mechanics, or industry itself—the working out of one's own personality, one's own inventiveness through forms of activity that are directly social—as all these activities are directly social—gives a man, through his very sociality, through the feeling he has that, as a good workman, he is cooperating with all other good workmen, a life interest apart from his rewards," he concluded.[6]

An academician, who is a Nobel Prize winner, addressed himself to this problem in a talk before an alumni group of his institution:

To ask the scientist or the scientific community to make all political, social, and economic judgements in a science-conditioned world may lead to disaster for democratic institutions. The scientist should inform the body of men about the scientific facts that are involved. The moral, political, and social judgements that must be made are the obligation of all men.[7]

After she had interviewed sixty-four eminent scientists, Anne Roe had some thoughts on the value problem that are worth noting:

Scientists are not super-human in their motivations. A few social scientists became so primarily in an attempt to work out a desire to be of service to others, but I do not find any evidence of such motivation in any of the other scientists, and it is relatively rare even among the psychologists in the group. This leads me to comment upon the opinion, held by many people, that the scientist is a completely altruistic being, devoting himself selflessly to the pursuit of truth, solely in order to contribute to the welfare of humanity. I do not intend it as a derogation of men whom I cherish when I say that this is, in my experience, not really the basic motivation for any of them, and as additional motivation it is more often absent than present. That they do, in fact, expend themselves in activities which are a very real contribution to humanity is the good luck of the society.[8]

Between the extremes of those who believe that scientists have a special role to play to advance social values and those who believe that the scientist's job is to provide the immediately useful because our culture requires it, there lies a middle ground that reaches out in both directions. Concern that the unchecked use of the scientific method will produce grave dangers for a world that is overly immersed in materialism and commercialism has been voiced by many thoughtful observers. One of the world's greatest scientists reflected on the problem of the scientific community and its values for the world in which we live when he asked and answered his own question:

What hopes and fears does the scientific method imply for mankind? I do not think that this is the right way to put the question. Whatever this tool in the hand of man will produce depends entirely on the nature of the goals alive in this mankind. Once these goals exist, the scientific method itself would not have led anywhere, it would not even have been born without a passionate striving for clear understanding. Perfections of means and confusion of goals seem—in my opinion—to characterize our age. If we desire sincerely and passionately the safety, the welfare, and the free development of the talents of all men, we shall not be in want of the means to approach such a state.[9]

The evidence in this study suggests that social scientists in industry realize that there is a conflict between perfection of means and confusion of goals, as Albert Einstein pointed out, and this conflict does impinge upon their own goals and careers. They agree, however, with the references cited above that it is not up to the individual scientist to determine the society's goals; this is a matter for the society to decide. At the same time, they do strive passionately for clear understanding in the sense of applying their talents to the solution of those problems that are placed before them, or that they think need attention for the continued growth of the organizations in which they work.

There is a tendency on the part of academicians to look with disdain upon those who engage in applied research, especially when the purpose is to bring about optimum return on private investment. William F. Whyte, an academician, took issue with such attitudes on the part of his social science colleagues who limit themselves to basic research:

> We hear much discussion of basic versus applied research. This seems to me a false dichotomy. I would rather divide the general area of research into three categories. One I would call "service research" or "information gathering." Another type is commonly called "basic research" with no thought of practical application. This approach leaves much to be desired by business. I suspect that it retreats from reality rather than facing the problem. The third approach has to be established on the basis of some proved payoff, and this approach requires both basic and applied research.

Whyte admitted that the third approach seemed like a contradiction in terms but in support of his view quoted from Chester Barnard's criticism of a report by the National Science Foundation that makes a distinction between basic and applied research. Barnard cited the work of Karl Jansky's discovery of radio signals from outer space while working on applied research, and Louis Pasteur's great contributions to the foundations of bacteriology in trying to find solutions to the practical problems of the silk and wine industries as examples of the inseparability of basic and applied research.[10]

In this age of tremendous and rapid change, contributions that can be made by social scientists to a better understanding of the world in which we live have hardly begun. Basic research in the social sciences has been neglected by industry and not given much support by the government through the National Science Foundation as compared with physical and life sciences. There are indications, however, that there is a growing appreciation of the practical value of the social sciences for, as Samuel Stouffer has noted, business is spending many millions of dollars annually in application of research findings to marketing, public relations, and personnel.[11]

The careers of social scientists in industry will be enhanced when the graduate schools of business in America fully implement the recommendation made by Robert Gordon and James Howell, who studied present courses offered in such schools, that "of all the subjects which he might undertake to study formally, none is more appropriate for the businessman-to-be than human behavior . . . by human behavior we mean most of the suject matter of the fields of psychology, sociology, and cultural anthropology."[12] A leading sociologist has asserted that the sale of industrial sociology to the manufacturing corporation may make the previous sale of rural sociology to the agricultural experiment stations appear as a minor transaction.[13] Finally, it must be pointed out that Ph.D.'s in the social sciences, as well as in other sciences, will be called upon more and more to take on administrative responsibilities in their fields. A survey of 10,000 Ph.D.'s in the sciences conducted by the National Academy of Sciences–National Research Council showed that the most spectacular trend was the rapid growth of administrative responsibility, chiefly at the expense of time used for research. Their report stated that twenty-five years after the doctorate, administration occupied the greatest single sector of time of the doctorate holders.[14]

CONCLUSION

Not less than two-thirds of social scientists in industry today expect to stay in that sector of the economy in the foreseeable future. Relatively few intend to leave private industry in the next ten years. Only the economists have a strong leaning toward leaving research and moving into positions of general management.

Those social scientists who might consider a move to another company would not give undue emphasis to a salary increase, although this factor would receive some weight. The most important considerations would be given to opportunities to work on difficult and challenging problems, to grow in their professions, and to learn new knowledge and skills. They would seek opportunities to make fuller use of their training with the understanding that they would have considerable freedom to carry out their own ideas on problems of central importance to the organization.

Statisticians would look for all of the above opportunities and, in addition, would want to work in organizations where they would have colleagues with high technical competence, and to have the respect of such colleagues.

From the data we have examined in this chapter, we may conclude that there are three types of career thinkers among social scientists now in private enterprise:

1. Those who are industry-minded, are greatly satisfied by their present career possibilities, and intend to pursue them in the organizations in which they are now employed. They are a majority of all social scientists in industry.

2. Those who want to continue their careers in industry but believe that they will have greater opportunities for more fruitful careers in another company.

3. Those who feel that the world of private enterprise is not for them. They expect to leave the industrial world to pursue their careers in other sectors of the economy.

We have heard from those in the first two categories as to the specific satisfactions or lack of them in their careers in industry. We turn now to the social scientists who left private enterprise to find out why they took this step. Are they older or younger than those who stay? Were their career changes brought about by the nature of the organizations in which they worked? Were their satisfactions and dissatisfactions while in industry the same or different from those of the social scientists who stayed?

Are there any circumstances or conditions under which the leavers would want to return to full-time careers in industry? These are the kinds of questions we shall be addressing in the next chapter to those who gave up careers in private enterprise.

WHY SOME SOCIAL SCIENTISTS
LEAVE INDUSTRY

8

In the preceding chapters we have established the fact that, by and large, social scientists in industry are well satisfied with their careers. There were some, however, who decided to leave private enterprise. Why did they leave? Did dissatisfactions outweigh satisfactions? Were career prospects poor? Are there any aspects of work outside of industry more attractive to certain social scientists? What about the age factor—were those who left older than those who stayed? Younger? About the same age? These are the kinds of questions that arose as the research was planned.

In this chapter we shall be making some comparisons between the "stayers" and the "leavers" in order to provide answers to the questions above, so that we may have a rounded picture of the motivational forces associated with a career in industry of highly educated social scientists.

METHODOLOGY

The directories of the professional associations were consulted to obtain the raw data. A span of at least five years was used in each category to locate those members who had been in industry and whose present addresses indicated that they were no longer associated with private companies. This procedure entailed making comparisons of about two thousand names of those listed in industry in 1963, and who were in academic, government, or non-profit organizations in 1968. Questionnaires were sent to those individuals who were working in such institutions. About ten per cent were interviewed. The response was very gratifying; sixty per cent replied, which is about the same order of return as was experienced with respondents who are still in industry.

HOW MANY LEFT INDUSTRY

Just under 100 social scientists left industry. This is about 5 per cent of the total found by the comparison of addresses as described above. Since the changes occurred in a period of five years, this percentage figure shows a remarkably low order of job change among social scientists with doctoral degrees who decided to undertake industrial careers.

The number who left industry was distributed as follows:

Psychologists	51
Economists	35
Statisticians	8
Sociologists	3
	97

	Number listed in the 1968 Register of Ph.D.s in industry	Number who left industry	Per cent
Psychologists	1001	51	5.1
Economists	405	35	8.6
Statisticians	151	8	5.3
Sociologists	35	3	8.3
	1592	97	6.1

The over-all average on a weighted basis as computed above leads us to the conclusion that a very small percentage of Ph.D. social scientists leave industry after they have embarked on professional careers in private enterprise.

WHERE THEY WENT TO CONTINUE THEIR CAREERS

Of those who left industry, eight out of ten accepted positions in academic institutions. The remainder were about equally divided between government and non-profit organizations.

The social scientists who elected to enter or re-enter academic life did so at highest ranks in colleges and universities. Two-thirds of them are now full professors, and almost one in five became a dean or assistant dean.

In government and non-profit organizations, transfers were to positions of about the same rank as held in industry, that is, department heads, research directors, or members of technical staffs, with equivalent titles after the change.

Some Comparisons Between Stayers and Leavers

	Per cent	
Present ages (1968)	Stayers	Leavers
under 33	1	0
33 to 37	5	20
38 to 42	24	20
43 to 47	29	24
48 to 52	24	20
53 to 57	10	13
58 to 62	6	3
63 and over	1	0
	100	100
up to 43	30	40
43 and over	70	60

Although it appears that those who left industry were slightly younger than those who stayed, the statistical differences in percentage terms are not significant. We might have assumed that those who left industry were either very much younger or were approaching that time when retirement from industry had to be faced. Obviously, such assumptions were not supported by the data above.

Employment at Ph.D.

	Per cent	
To	*Stayers*	*Leavers*
Industry	50	55
College or universities	32	25
Government	8	15
Non-profit organizations	10	5
	100	100

There are only minor percentage differences in the types of employment at the time of receiving the Ph.D. of the respondents when we compare those who are still in industry and those who left. Again the data were somewhat unexpected. We might have assumed, for example, that since eight out of ten of those who left industry went to positions in academia, a comparable number would have had that experience before entering industry. We see from the data above that only a quarter of the respondents had such experience. Obviously, the kind of employment experience prior to leaving private enterprise was not a major factor in the decision to leave.

SALARY BEFORE LEAVING INDUSTRY AND
SALARY NOW

The respondents were asked to indicate total yearly earnings at present, and total remuneration received in the last job in industry. The comparison follows:

	Per cent	
	Present	Last job in industry
Up to $10,000 per year	0	9
Over $10,000 to $15,000	15	40
Over $15,000 to $20,000	29	24
Over $20,000	56	27
	100	100

The salary data were quite unexpected. This writer assumed that academic pay would not begin to compare with compensation rates offered by industry. There are a number of possible explanations, but before undertaking to analyze the table above, it would be valuable to have some knowledge on levels in the organizations that were held by the respondents before they left industry.

**Managerial Level at Time of Leaving
Compared With Level of Stayers**

	Per cent	
	Stayers	Leavers
Top Management	26	11
Middle Management	36	18
Bottom Management	38	71
	100	100

We now have before us some very revealing figures. Quite obviously, those who left industry were, for the most part, in much lower positions than those who remained in industrial jobs. These data, together with the salary information previously given, indicates a fairly sharp demarcation between those social scientists who expect to continue their careers in industry and those who left such positions. The reader may recall from Chapter 1 that over half of all social scientists now in industry were receiving $20,000 or more per year, whereas only a quarter of those who left were in the same top salary category and a half were paid from $10,000 to $15,000 per year. Only 15 per cent of the stayers were in this salary range.

The conclusion seems obvious, but we should have two more pieces of information before coming to a final conclusion and those are: (1) did the leavers have significantly shorter service in industry, and (2) were they job hoppers? The answer to both questions is interesting. Both the stayers and the leavers had about the same length of service, a median of ten years for the stayers and eight years for the leavers, and the largest number in each category had worked in two companies.

We can now conclude that those who left, in addition to any other dissatisfactions that they may have had, were lower down in the managerial hierarchy, paid less well, and must have been somewhat ambivalent about whether to stay or leave. When a university offered higher pay than they were receiving in industry, and top faculty positions, the pull was very strong. When we examine the data to follow together with their written comments we shall see that those who left industry did not take this action hurriedly nor with a feeling of great dislike for their industrial jobs. About half of those who left, when asked if they would like to return, replied in the affirmative. As we shall see, pay and status were not the predominant reasons for leaving industry.

WHY THEY ACCEPTED EMPLOYMENT IN INDUSTRY

After reviewing the notes made during the interviews, and re-reading the write-in comments supplied by the respondents who left industry, it was concluded that the reasons given by the leavers were very similar to those given by the stayers as shown in Chapter 4. The reader may recall that opportunity, challenge, freedom to do research, and good salary were all prominently mentioned. In other words, it was difficult to find any reasons for accepting employment in industry by those who left later that were markedly different from the ones given by those who stayed.

COMPARISONS ON WORK ASPECTS

There were a number of questions asked of the respondents still in industry that were also administered to those who left so that differences, if any, in their feelings or reactions toward various aspects of work could be determined. In the tables that follow, we shall be looking for such differences. The first question had to do with autonomy. Although phrased in somewhat different terms, the essence of the question was the same:

Q. During the time you were employed full-time in industry, to what extent did you have autonomy to determine your own program in contrast to having work assigned by management?

	Per cent	
Amount of Autonomy	Stayers	Leavers
Nil to moderate	25	39
Substantial	55	48
Complete	20	13
	100	100

Q. When new and important ideas occurred to you, how easily could you get them across to other people in the organization who might have been affected by them?

	Per cent	
Ease of Communicating Ideas	Stayers	Leavers
Difficult to mixed	36	73
Fairly easy	41	23
Very easy	23	4
	100	100

Q. Some individuals are completely involved in their professional work—absorbed in it night and day. For others, their work is simply one of several interests. When you were in industry, how involved did you feel in your work?

Per cent		
Amount of Involvement	*Stayers*	*Leavers*
Not much, slightly or moderately	14	26
Strongly	35	36
Very strongly, completely	51	38
	100	100

Q. How important do you think your work was in industry, that is, how much of a contribution did it make to either basic knowledge or application in your professional field?

Per cent		
Importance of Work	*Stayers*	*Leavers*
Of no, slight, or moderate importance	24	49
Substantial	36	20
Very substantial, utmost	40	31
	100	100

As we review the percentage comparisons in the four questions above, differences in two aspects stand out quite sharply: (1) those who left industry had a very difficult time getting new ideas across to people in the organization who might be affected by them, and (2) many more of the leavers felt that their work in industry was not making much of a contribution to basic knowledge in their fields than did those who are still in private enterprise. These two factors, if negative, are powerful forces in frustrating self-actualizing individuals, especially those who are highly educated and trained.

Additional dissatisfaction came from two other sources and, although not of the same order of significance, they nevertheless combined with the two already mentioned to create sufficient restiveness for those who ultimately left to do so. The leavers seemed to have less autonomy in their work than those who stayed in industry; and those who left did not feel that they had as much professional involvement in their work as did those still in private enterprise.

One more comparison between the stayers and leavers was made possible by this question:

Q. As you think back on your industrial experience, how important was it to you to appear well in the eyes of those listed? The numbers in each column are the weighted averages obtained by the following scoring system:

None-0   Slight-1   Moderate-2   Great-3   Utmost-4

	Per cent	
Person or unit	Stayers	Leavers
Your immediate superior	2.97	2.81
Higher management in your field	2.47	2.57
Top executives in the company	2.49	2.17
Departments using your work	2.66	2.61
Professional colleagues in the company	2.48	2.42
Professional colleagues outside of the company	2.34	1.94

Again we note that there are few differences in the feelings of those who left as compared with those who stayed in the rankings given to persons or groups who judged the work or reputations of the respondents. Those who left did not regard top executives in the company as being too important for appraisal of their work. It was surprising, however, to find that the leavers gave bottom ranking to professional colleagues outside the company just as did those who stayed. We might have assumed that the social scientists who had thoughts of leaving might have had some concern about how they appeared professionally in the eyes of colleagues, particularly outside of industry, but such was not the case with the respondents in this study.

HOW THE LEAVERS SAW THEIR CAREERS
WHILE IN INDUSTRY

A question was asked of those who left in order to get some indication of how the respondents viewed their careers while they were in private enterprise. Did they see themselves essentially as professionals mainly interested in their fields of science or did they think about opportunities for moving up in their organizations? The next table provides us with some insight on this aspect of their thinking.

Q. When you were in industry, how did you think about your career in the organization?

	Per cent
An opportunity to do important professional work.	37
An opportunity to stay in my field but to manage the activities rather than do them.	15
An opportunity to get involved in other activities of the organization as well as in my field in order to prepare for or accept greater responsibilities.	41
An opportunity to move out of my field and get into a top executive position in the organization.	7
	100

The results above are interesting, for they indicate that there was about an even split between those who wanted to limit themselves to their particular fields of science and those who had ideas beyond that limitation. This finding is in consonance with what has been previously indicated about the leavers that, after they left industry, quite a few became deans, chairmen of departments, or directors of research in government or non-profit organizations who must be action-oriented from an administrative point of view. The experience gained in industry apparently carried over into their new positions.

WHY THEY LEFT INDUSTRY

We come now to the key question asked of the leavers—why they left industry. It was quite difficult to sort the responses into discrete categories. However, the writer used the same method of sorting as had been used previously with the stayers in presenting data regarding gratifications or lack of them. It should be stated, before giving the percentage tabulations of reasons for leaving, that the leavers were also asked to state what aspects of work in industry were most gratifying. The writer found few significant differences between the responses of the stayers and the leavers. In general, it can be said that the write-in responses of those who stayed and those who left were about the same. There were many positive gratifications expressed by the leavers, but with one major exception: pay or level in the organization did not appear nearly as often in the responses of the leavers as in those of the stayers.

Reasons Given for Leaving Industry

	Per cent
Wanted to enter academic life, or return to teaching	30
Pay better in new position	28
New poistion offered more challenge	25
Job insecurity; lack of tenure	22
Limited opportunity to make contributions to his field of science	15
Conflict of values	15
Wanted to move to an academic community; dislike of regular hours, or travel to work	12
Dislike of superiors	2
Nearing retirement	2

NOTE: Column adds up to more than 100 per cent, as respondents gave more than one reason.

The figures above have definite value for our later analysis, but we shall be able to derive much more insight from reading the actual responses from which the above data were obtained. Every write-in comment is important for fuller understanding of the motivations of those who left industry. However, selections were made so as to avoid repetitious replies.

WRITE-IN COMMENTS

By Economists

I wasn't on my way up in the organization. I had given myself 5 years to see how far I could get in industry, and by the end of that time, found myself stuck in a staff job that wasn't very satisfying. Since I had originally worked for a Ph.D. to prepare for college teaching, I decided to leave industry after teaching part-time at a university and found the experience vastly more satisfying.

An outstanding opportunity came along to head a university research center with complete freedom to undertake the kind of research I always wanted to do. I didn't leave the company because of any negative factors, but because the new opportunity broadened my professional scope.

There were increasing pressures on me to become a "businessman" and fewer opportunities to be a professional economist.

I wanted to return to my home state and get my family away from urban living. I was offered an opportunity to reorganize the School of Business at the state university and this, combined with my family's wishes, produced the decision to leave.

The company's liberal benefit program made it possible for me to continue to live in the style to which I had become accustomed. With our children all on their own, and a strong desire to go into academic life, I made the change.

I liked teaching and research better (based on my "moonlighting") and disliked the pathologies and dysfunctions of the industrial bureaucracy. I particularly resented the internal politics and the poor appointments to key positions. Pay, hours, and the physical building were great, but the unprofessional milieu counterbalanced these. Since we all periodically take stock of ourselves, and we don't live forever, why put up with the guff and settle for less than is available in a university?

After two frustrating years at the company where I last worked, I found that my department was not going to offer me the professional opportunities that had been outlined for me when I was hired. I decided a radical change was needed—not just a transfer to another part of the company but an opportunity to develop my own ideas. I thought this could best be done in an academic environment.

The challenge of being asked to organize and administer a new basic research organization designed to serve both business and academic communities caused me to leave in order to participate in the development of a young, growing, and highly motivated university.

An attractive academic opportunity came my way at a time when I felt that I had learned about as much as I was going to from industry experience. I also felt that I had gotten about as high on the promotion ladder as I was going to. My position made me more of an auxiliary than a principal actor in the main activities.

By Psychologists

As I approached 50, I felt that my life pattern was not very satisfying at this stage of life. I had been thinking of returning to university life—I had 5 years of it before spending the next 15 in an industrial position—and so when a good university offer came along, I took it.

A number of factors combined at about the same time that made the decision to leave an easy one. The company I was working for started a strong economy drive that resulted in a reduction in the number of interesting problems that could be researched. After several years of doing about the same kind of work, and the fact that university salaries had moved up to be attractive enough to consider, I decided I had had enough of industry.

My new job with a non-profit organization has given me much greater freedom to deal with important problems that have real significance for the society. The pay is just as good, and I have less of a feeling that I am "owned" by the organization.

I was called to active duty with the Air Force during the Berlin crisis of 1962. On returning, I decided to take a government job because of many internal changes in the company that I worked for, and the instability of contract-based assignments. In addition, my wife disliked the isolation, my frequent and lengthy absences from home, and the prospects of more moving if I stayed with the company.

An extremely atractive offer came from a university, attractive in salary, kind of work, and colleagues, just at the time that there was a re-organization of the research department to a very bureaucratic structure. I no longer had the freedom and stimulation of the early years with the company; I felt that I could learn very little by staying, and I found business *mores* confining. I couldn't work up any enthusiasm about improving sales in a large financial institution.

I got caught in a mass cutback when the company re-organized. I had always been interested in living and working overseas, and when a government agency offered me a job to do media and opinion research, which was pretty close to the kind of work I was in at the time in an advertising agency, I decided to move. Although I found the advertising business interesting and enjoyed the people in it very much, I had gotten quite concerned about the world situation and what I could do about it. The move out of industry into government satisfied that urge.

I never intended to stay in industry. My original plan called for me to try it for about three years and then return to industry. However, I became fascinated by the adventure, intrigue, and the money, and had three different jobs in 12 years. By then I'd had it and came back to academic life.

In an industrial organization, one works for the company and not for one's self. I decided, after three different jobs in industry, that I wanted to be my own boss and combine teaching with consulting. I could determine where I wanted to live and not be subject to corporate influence, transfer, or being fired. In addition, business mergers create a feeling of instability in private enterprise.

I was miserable working for a tyrant; I hated his authority and his pettiness. I love psychology and wanted to make much fuller use of my Ph.D. training, to teach, do research, and to write. The university gives me all of these opportunities.

Although some of my work was highly satisfying and, in my opinion, socially constructive, too much of my work was of little or no consequence except to increase some company's profit margin. I have nothing against that, nor do I oppose the business system, but I did not want to devote my whole career to these objectives.

I was 27, no longer starving, and viewed my job as not involved with anything significant. The university offered a chance to do something significant, and I accepted a teaching position despite an initially punishing income cut.

I had an excellent opportunity to continue the same line of research in a highly respected university in association with colleagues that I admired. The almost 5 years in industry had been rewarding and productive, but I felt that I would be happier in an academic atmosphere with greater freedom of action and opportunities for teaching.

By Sociologists

When I started in industry, I had a real good opportunity to learn about and develop research skills in a heretofore little explored area: Human group-complex machine interface. In addition, I was attracted by what seemed to be a much more flexible work situation, more professional freedom and, of course, a markedly superior salary. The freedom and the salary materialized, but the remainder of my expectations were not. It was obvious that I should go back to academic life, and when such an opportunity came along, I took it.

First, I found the chronic instability of the aerospace industry a source of anxiety. The constant spectre of termination made me uneasy. Second, I found it difficult to visualize a career route for myself in either of the aerospace firms I worked for which was partly due to the inherent instability of the industry. It also related to the fact that these organizations are structured so that the social scientist simply has no place to go unless he divests himself of his identity as a social scientist. As one or more of my "successful" colleagues put it: "I am a *former* sociologist." Third, I have had continuous doubts about a career which I call the "destructive artists and scientists." Does a social scientist have any place in an organization that manufactures weapons and devices for war? I think not.

The organization was concerned with practical matters and not much with research in my field. My main interest is research and so I left.

By Statisticians

My first love has always been teaching. I found that I wanted to get back to university life not so much for research, but to get back to teaching. With my children nearly on their own, less strain on the bank account, and with an offer to return with a full professorship, I left industry.

I could no longer accept the pay for making practically no contribution and having even less interest in my job.

There was no real reason to be creative. Ideas were usually squelched early.

I didn't like the way funds would be suddenly cut off with no relation to performance, but solely on the basis of expediency. The university offered me a more challenging job.

ANALYSIS OF WRITE-IN COMMENTS

The richness of the material presented here made it difficult for the writer to neatly categorize the comments. The reader will no doubt perceive that a number of strains run through a great many of the statements. Quite obviously, the respondents were ready for change for a variey of reasons. In many cases it was not a matter of liking industrial careers less, but nonindustrial opportunities, especially in universities, were liked more. The combination of being offered top ranks, good pay— in many cases better than in industry—and elimination of anxiety over job security because of organizational changes or mergers were strong extrinsic factors. Equally strong were the intrinsic ones that resulted from desires to engage in teaching in universities or to return to academic life, the opportunities to undertake new responsibilities and see their ideas implemented, and a feeling that the very nature of some businesses militated against personal values—especially in companies involved with weaponry—were all powerful forces that came into action when a university position was offered.

Career change should be differentiated from job hopping. In the case of the respondents, both the stayers and the leavers, there was remarkable job stability. It must be considered that the median age in both groups was about forty-five, at which point a change in career is not undertaken lightly. Those who stayed realized that they must build internal reputations, a time-consuming effort in any organization, especially for social scientists. Fred Goldner found that the sociological literature on roles—despite its volume—did not help him very much in understanding either his job or the organization as a whole when he became a full-time employee of a large corporation.[1]

A major source of frustration for the respondents who left industry was their apparent inability to communicate effectively with higher management and those who might be affected by their research studies. The reader may recall that in the case of the stayers this aspect was also a cause for dissatisfaction, especially for those in research laboratories. Daniel Roman has pointed out that in highly specialized research-and-development organizations, individual mobility is limited by compartmentalization; there is little crossing of functional lines, and it is difficult to establish communications and integrate operations.[2] There is a question here of cause and effect. Does the social scientist, working with physical scientists in most research laboratories, have communication difficulties because physical scientists tend to isolate themselves in their specialties, or does he become an isolate because there are few social scientists in laboratories? This is a difficult question to answer and requires much more research. We do know, however, that the respondents in this study were eager to get involved in central and important problems of their organizations and were disappointed when this did not happen.

Reference has already been made to the possibility of conflict between the social scientist's personal values and those of the organization. Citations were offered from a number of scientists that indicated the importance of separating values from scientific accomplishment. Some readers will, no doubt, bridle at the suggestion that personal values should be set aside in the interests of scientific advancement. Such a suggestion is not being made. As a matter of fact, we have seen in some of the write-in comments in this chapter that such conflicts were important reasons for some individuals to leave industry. It is interesting, however, that only 15 per cent of the respondents included this reason in their comments.

Of considerable significance is the fact that virtually none of the respondents left because of personal difficulties with their superiors. The leavers, like the stayers, gave the highest ranking to their immediate organization superiors when asked to rate the importance they gave to persons or units who were in a position to appraise their work.

It is fair to conclude that there is a strong likelihood that the leavers were never really certain that they wanted a lifetime career in industry. When circumstances arose that triggered this feeling into a career change, the change took place. Obviously, the stayers were probably faced with similar situations. Their reactions resulted in looking for new jobs in industry or finding ways to be transferred to other units in the same organization. The stayers intended to stay in private enterprise.

HOW THE LEAVERS FEEL ABOUT RETURNING TO INDUSTRY

We shall conclude this chapter by asking the respondents whether they would ever return to industry. This question was included as the final one in the questionnaire in order to test present feelings after industrial experience. It was assumed that if feelings were hostile or embittered the replies would reflect such attitudes.

Just about half of the respondents replied in the affirmative when asked: "Are there any circumstances or conditions under which you would want to return to full-time employment in industry?" It should be interesting to the reader to examine the circumstances and conditions under which the respondents would return; these responses also were quite revealing in determining why some social scientists leave industry.

WRITE-IN COMMENTS OF THOSE WHO WOULD RETURN

An economist, now chairman of his department at a state university, replied:

Certainly. The work was most interesting and extremely important socially. I genuinely enjoyed it, but salaries in corporate management are no longer competitive with those in academia. There has also been a tendency for corporations to skimp on their upper management in order to keep costs down while satisfying labor union demands for production personnel. To reverse an old saw, I can't afford the pleasures of corporate life.

An associate professor of economics at another state university thought he would consider returning to industry but not to a situation like the one he left for his present position. He wrote:

Clearly, there are many companies that provide work that meets the conditions that I had been led to expect at the company I left. Should my present highly satisfactory situation change, and I sought a new job, I would examine industrial as well as academic positions. For what it is worth, my limited exposure through job interviews and consulting work is that government is markedly inferior to academic and business organizations as an employer.

An industrial psychologist, now a professor at a large university, wrote that he would consider returning to industry—where he spent fifteen years and rose to an important staff position—if he ever became disenchanted with academic life, but only to a situation where he felt he could make a significant contribution as a social scientist.

Another industrial psychologist, who is now professor of marketing at a "name" university, would return to industry as research director in a large company that provided new challenges, and more stability in its funding of social science research than the company he left after nine years for university life.

A Ph.D. whose specialty was Learning responded to the question with some qualifications that revealed his feelings about working in a profit-oriented company. (He is now a social scientist in a government-based organization.) He wrote:

Yes, I would return if the company seemed to offer the best possibility for developing instructional systems of the interactive variety, that is, computer-based. However, even the best corporations apparently want every development to show a profit in at least three years. The publicity about industry investing in instructional technology is, in my opinion, almost completely a lot of wind. They simply do not see that a lot of research and development is necessary, and since there is very little leadership from industry to engage in such research, a vacuum exists. Either industry should admit, with candor, that profit-oriented enterprise is not geared for undertaking projects with moderate pay-off possibilities or stop all the public relations nonsense.

A professor of statistics, who had been director of reliability research at a large aerospace company for a number of years, wrote:

At times I wish I could be back in industry, not because of the higher salary that I used to have, but because I miss knowing what is going on in the space programs. Also, the *prima donna* attitude of some of the university faculty is annoying, but don't get me wrong; there are a lot of wonderful people in academic life.

A sociologist who had been employed in an aircraft manufacturing company, and is now an associate professor at a state
university, set forth a number of conditions that he would require before he considered returning to industry. He wrote:

I would be happy to have another full-time job in industry under
the following conditions: (1) That the organization is not engaged
in the development or manufacture of products for war; (2) That I
could maintain a clear identity as a professional person in the organization; (3) That a definite career route was visible and open for
me; (4) That the organization is not only stable but growing; (5)
That the salary and fringe benefits were satisfactory; (6) That my
work would allow me freedom of judgement and action as a responsible professional.

The dean of a school of business, formerly director of economic research at a very large bank, commented that he would
consider returning to industry providing the assignment was a
challenging one with clear-cut authority to do the job the way
he thought it should be done. "However," he wrote, "I now
own part of a consulting company that gives me a good outlet
for my compulsiveness to run other people's businesses, and the
present combination of academic and part-time business is
probably best for me."

Another dean who is also director of a research institute at a
large university wrote:

I would have no objection to it at all. At this point in time, it
would have to be in a managerial position and not a technical or
professional staff job as I am really pretty far removed from current
practice in my present position. Except that I am in an academic
setting and my work is with academic people, I see little difference
between my present position and say that of a branch manager of a
major corporation.

A third dean, whose Ph.D. was in psychology, replied that it
was conceivable but highly unlikely that he would ever return
to full-time employment in industry. However, if he was offered

a position where he would have the opportunity to attack significant social inadequacies in the society, he would consider such a move "because," he wrote, "I think industry is now as vigorous and creative in working on social problems as academic institutions are."

A number of replies were somewhat facetious, posing conditions for return that the respondent knew would not be met such as a very high position in management, with a large salary, profit-sharing, and complete freedom to do as he wished.

WRITE-IN COMMENTS OF THOSE WHO WOULD NOT RETURN

Most of the negative replies were quite terse with such words as "no," "never," or "I can't imagine this happening." A few, however, were revealing of feelings behind the attitudes indicated, and so have been included for their possible worth to aid our analysis.

This response, from a professor of industrial relations and associate director of the university's industrial relations center, left little doubt about his feelings:

No, I would not return under any circumstances. I am constantly being approached by head hunters offering lush jobs and pushed by former colleagues who hear about openings that are in the $35,-000 to $40,000 range that they think I should consider. I like teaching and research and have all the money I need. I think the creation and dissemination of knowledge are more important than fighting the pettyfogging battles of industrial relations in a corporate bureaucracy. I would consider taking a one-year leave of absence now and then to work in industry or government to recapture the reality dimension periodically, but I think I'd just as soon face a firing squad more happily than spend the rest of my life in the glass house of corporate headquarters. Moreover, in my present job I have an ideal mixture of university-based activity with industry involvement.

An industrial psychologist, who spent five years in industry and is now on leave from a university where he is a professor of psychology in order to do some research for a government agency, wrote:

If you mean return to profit-based industry, the answer is definitely no. Selling products, making better cameras, or other materialistic production, is no longer of any importance in my value system. On the other hand, working for non-profit organizations such as the one I'm with now, is definitely of interest to me.

An associate professor of psychology wrote that he would not consider returning to industry "because I can have my cake and eat it too. I can be active as a teacher and researcher and be a consultant too. I can earn more money this way than as a full-time employee."

An associate dean of a school of business at a state university replied that he could think of no circumstances under which he might return to industry. He explained: "Since joining academia, I have never been so happy in my life nor done such significant work!"

A professor of business administration doubted that he would ever return to industry. After seven years at a prestigious university in the east, he spent the next fourteen years in industry, the last ten in one of the country's largest consulting firms where he held a top management position. He is now at a graduate school of business in a leading university and wrote, "I have come home to academic life."

CONCLUSION

Very few social scientists with doctoral degrees leave full-time employment in industry once they have undertaken professional careers in private enterprise. Even among those who leave industry many would return if offered the kinds of professional opportunities that did not fully materialize when they were employed full-time in the industrial sector of our economy.

The leavers exhibited the same general satisfactions and dissatisfactions reported by the stayers even though the former were not in as high positions while they were in industry as the latter. The combination of wanting to try academic life or return to it, higher salaries now being offered by universities, and elimination of job insecurity, were all powerful forces that produced desires for career change. The most powerful, however, were the intrinsic feelings that jobs outside of industry would produce opportunities to do more creative work, to contribute in greater measure to new knowledge, and reduce or eliminate conflict of personal values with industrial goals.

According to Dr. H. Buyford Stever, President of Carnegie-Mellon University, there is a prospect of a growing shortage of Ph.D.'s for industry because of cutbacks in government research grants and increasing pressures to draft college graduates before they undertake Ph.D. studies. If the cuts in funds for research continue over a long term, Dr. Stever believes that the ability of universities to produce researchers for industry will diminish.[3] Although Dr. Stever probably had in mind a reduction in the number of physical scientists, it is likely that his warning applies equally to social scientists. This admonition clearly requires that all sectors of the economy must, if they have not already done so, create conditions that will result in optimum utilization of this scarce and precious human resource in our society—our highly educated and trained scientists who have committed themselves to professional careers because such work fulfills their innermost desires to be of value to the society in which they live.

In the final chapter, we shall summarize our findings based on the research reported here and draw some conclusions as to how the services professional social scientists can be administered so as to create maximum satisfaction for the scientist and the organization for which he works.

SUMMARY OF MAJOR FINDINGS: IMPLICATIONS FOR MANAGEMENT

9

The primary purpose of this book has been to present and analyze research data gathered from a random sample of social scientists employed full-time in American industry in order to understand from their perceptions their roles, their motivations, and how they view their careers as professionals. The knowledge gained should contribute to a better understanding of how the services of such highly educated people should be administered so that the individuals and the organizations in which they work will both benefit. This final chapter, then, will be devoted to summarizing what we have discovered from the interviews, questionnaire responses, and the write-in comments, and what implications can be adduced for personnel administration of social scientists in industry. A reasonable way to begin is to restate the questions raised in the first chapter and supply the answers from the data analysis.

1. *How and when did social scientists decide on their future careers? Did those now in industry have such careers in mind early in their collegiate years?*

Fewer than half of the future social scientists had a definite occupational goal in mind when they entered college. However, the fact that at least four out of ten said that they did have an occupational goal at this stage in their lives indicates a stronger propensity toward early goal determination than one usually finds in high school graduates. It is common experience that the largest number who enter college have vague ideas as to the kinds of careers they really want to follow. Although many youngsters select a major field of study, largely because the college requires that such a decision be made—usually by the sophomore year—the sparse data that have been published show that there is little correlation between these decisions and later careers. In the case of professionals, however, the career decision is usually quite firm by the time of the baccalaureate, since graduate studies must be undertaken in order to prepare for such careers.

In the case of social scientists, almost ninety per cent of them said they had definite occupational goals by the time they had acquired the doctorate. Their choices at that time were roughly divided into almost equal thirds of wanting to be college teachers, do research in their fields in industry, and being undecided about the kinds of organizations in which they wanted to work. Almost none wanted positions in government or non-profit organizations. Although all of the respondents eventually accepted employment in industry, at the time of the Ph.D. a third did go to teaching careers in colleges or universities, about ten per cent went into government research departments, and an equal number into non-profit organizations. The remainder, just under half in the research population, went to industry.

In response to the question whether they had industrial careers in mind early in their collegiate years, the answer was negative. Only a minority felt that they wanted to work in industry when they entered upon their college studies. Even by the time of the Ph.D. only a third definitely wanted industrial careers.

Paul Lazarsfeld has pointed out that a majority of the sociologists teaching in American liberal arts colleges have an ideological bias against industry. "Aiding the doctor, promoting justice, or supporting the agencies of the law—all these are in accord with accepted norms; helping the businessman make money is not," he wrote.[1] His observation was certainly sustained in this study; two-thirds of the sociologists with Ph.D.'s joined universities, government, or non-profit organizations on acquiring their doctorates. In the case of the other social sciences, however, the qualms about working in industry on completion of graduate studies subsided for more than half of them, especially the statisticians.

IMPLICATION FOR FUTURE AVAILABILITY FOR EMPLOYMENT

If the trend shown by our data continues, industrial organizations will be favored as places to work by social scientists who have no special leaning toward academic life. Ph.D.'s in colleges and universities who are more interested in large-scale research than a combination of teaching and pecking away at small research projects with meager funds will be a major source for recruitment to fill industry's needs. Social scientists in government and non-profit organizations will also provide some candidates for employment in industry, but not to any great extent.

American industry cannot assume that social scientists with doctoral degrees will always favor positions in private enterprise over those available in academia, government, or non-profit organizations. Much depends on industry's ability to provide the kind of "climate of discovery" suggested by J. Douglas Brown, in which the main function of the administrator is to assure the creative scientist of his economic status and security so that his energies can be focused on his scientific accomplishments.[2]

2. *Do social scientists seek positions in industry primarily because of higher salaries than can be expected in government, universities, or non-profit organizations?*

The answer to this question is "no" if what we mean by "primarily" is that salary level overshadows all other considerations. Money is certainly an important consideration in the social scientist's decision as to where he wants to work, but it is not the most important. As we have seen, opportunity to use his Ph.D. training as a scientist together with a vision of considerable challenge to his intellectual ability in the kinds of problems he will be asked to grapple with, are very powerful forces to attract the social scientist with a Ph.D. degree to work in industry. This conclusion is sustained by the statistical data and even more by the write-in comments and interviews in which the reasons why social scientists accepted positions in industry were determined.

Salary levels in colleges and universities have moved up quite considerably over the last decade. The 1969–70 scales for a "Class A" university, on a 12-month basis, are as follows:

Rank	Range	Merit Maximum
Professor	$16,086 to $20,910	$26,538
Associate Professor	13,233 to 17,205	21,839
Assistant Professor	10,369 to 13,477	17,103

SOURCE: American Association of University Professors, Rutgers University Chapter

The most recent salary information for social scientists published by the National Science Foundation is based on 1968 data. It is possible, however, to make some comparisons between the various types of employers as shown in the following table:

Median Annual Salaries of Full-time Employed Civilian Scientists
with Ph.D. Degrees[3]

	Educational Institutions Calendar Year	Federal Government	Non-Profit Organizations	Industry and Business
All fields	$14,800	$15,800	$16,000	$17,500
Economists	16,800	19,000	20,500	23,800
Psychologists	15,000	15,800	15,000	19,000
Sociologists	15,000	18,300	16,600	25,000
Statisticians	16,200	20,200	19,000	19,200

The salaries reported by those who had been in industry and are now in universities indicate that the majority receive an annual salary of $20,000 or more as shown in the last chapter. We can conclude, therefore, that academic salaries have become quite competitive with the other employing organizations for social scientists with doctoral degrees. In addition, social scientists in academic institutions are often called upon by industry and other organizations as consultants. The most common fee is reported to be a minimum of $100 per day plus expenses.

IMPLICATIONS FOR RECRUITMENT AND
SALARY ADMINISTRATION

In past years, personnel managers have not paid much attention to salary scales in academic institutions because it was assumed that industry salaries were far above those paid to college and university teachers. This assumption no longer holds as the data show. Government and non-profit institutions have also raised their salary sights.

A young Ph.D. can usually be assured of being appointed to the rank of assistant professor in virtually all colleges and universities. Those who are academically inclined will not be concerned with industry salaries. The social scientists who prefer to do large-scale research and are not interested in teaching careers have enjoyed the result of competition among industry, government, and non-profit institutions for their services. Industry will certainly have to stay ahead in money terms in order to attract Ph.D.'s who are starting their careers or who want to move into private enterprise from outside of that sector of the economy.

3. *Do social scientists in industry have any desire to move into positions of line responsibility in their companies and away from professional careers in their fields of science?*

As we reviewed the data and write-in comments in Chapter 7, we saw that, except for economists, social scientists were mainly interested in professional careers in their fields. This finding included the fact that they expected to become managers of research groups and sought such opportunities because in higher staff positions they could become more highly involved in the decision-making processes in top-line management. A third of the economists are interested in general management positions, and such social scientists are to be found in top managerial posts in American industry. With the qualification that economists are somewhat different in their career desires than the other social scientists, we can reply to the question by saying, "No, they do not want to move into positions that will take them out of their fields."

IMPLICATION FOR MANAGEMENT DEVELOPMENT
PROGRAMS IN INDUSTRY

The typical approach to development of managerial resources by most industrial organizations is to use a combination of rotational assignments in two or more areas of the company together with sending promising individuals to advanced management training programs conducted by graduate schools of business such as Harvard, Columbia, Northwestern, Cornell, Pittsburgh, and Stanford, to name a few. The basic idea behind these programs is to convert specialists into generalists. Attempts have been made to measure the effects of such training on the individuals, but there are little hard data to support any conclusions because there are too many variables present in any given situation. Even if such programs succeeded in their objectives —and there is a little evidence to support such a conclusion— what would be the point in sending a competent social scientist to such programs if he had no desire to become a generalist, unless he was an economist and had requested such a career change? The organization would be better served if it encouraged scientists to nominate themselves for line management training instead of assuming, as is often the case, that everyone welcomes the opportunity to move into executive positions.

The respondents in this study clearly indicated that they were not interested in general management. Instead, it would be more profitable for the organization and the individual social scientists to provide ample opportunity for gaining competence. Attendance at professional meetings, and presentation of papers before colleagues in his field provide at least minimal opportunities for development and are quite common in most large organizations. More needs to be done such as encouraging social scientists to engage in part-time teaching at universities, to accept assignments to work with other scientists on research projects in the public interest including the granting of leaves of absence for such work. The introduction of sabbatics for such purposes has not been generally used in industry. This approach to professional development should be worth exploring.

4. *The majority of social scientists employed full-time in in-industry are to be found in large companies. It has been asserted by several writers that large corporations stifle individuality and creativity. Do social scientists in industry feel stifled and less creative than their colleagues outside of industry?*

Autonomy is closely related to individuality and creativity. Freedom, or the lack of it, to develop one's own approaches to solutions of problems, and to select those problems that are of the greatest challenge are good measures of autonomy. The respondents in this study, almost all of whom work in large companies, said that they had a considerable amount of freedom in their work. This was true regardless of type of science and, with the exception of research laboratories, existed in all types of organizations.

When we examined the reasons why some social scientists left industry to continue their careers in academic institutions, lack of autonomy in their industrial jobs was hardly mentioned as a cause for leaving. However, many did complain that they were not being given important problems to work on.

Another measure of how individuals feel about their work is how involved they feel. Obviously, if there is a high order of involvement, there is a strong likelihood that creativity is released. The respondents indicated that they were very strongly involved in their work.

IMPLICATIONS FOR CREATING OPTIMUM CONDITIONS FOR CREATIVITY

When higher management assigns problems to a social scientist and holds him responsible for providing professional guidance but limits his freedom to tackle the problems in the way that he deems best, the same kind of frustration can be expected as that experienced by a line manager who has been delegated responsibility but given little authority by the delegator.

The major motivation expressed by the respondents in this study for accepting positions in industry was the opportunity to work on important problems where their special training could be applied. If social scientists are given more and more routine and repetitive problems and fewer new and challenging ones, they will begin to look for opportunities outside the particular organization in which employed. An important measure of their worth to the organization was the amount of contact the respondents had with higher executives. Obviously, top managers could be expected to be grappling with the most important problems of the organization. If social scientists are called upon by the top men in the company to assist them by providing research data that will influence their decisions, their creative abilities will be strained to the utmost, a desirable condition for highly trained professionals in all fields. Donald Pelz and Frank Andrews reported that those scientists who were esteemed by their colleagues for their scientific contributions, and particularly for usefulness to the organization, reported excellent opportunities to use their skills and to carry out their own ideas. "The organizations we surveyed were good at recognizing high performers. They rewarded achievers with more freedom, interesting work, contact with executives, and better pay. . . . It might be argued that the provision of such factors—giving the individuals a chance to follow his own ideas, to tackle challenging problems, and to be appreciated by being paid well—actually helped to build a stimulating atmosphere in which individuals could do their best work," they wrote.[4]

The implications for management are quite clear. The evidence in this study fully confirms the findings made by Pelz and Andrews as well as other researchers that management can enhance or diminish the creativity of professionals by management's evaluation of the importance of the professionals' work, as shown through the nature of the problems that these highly trained individuals are called upon to help solve. At the same time, there must be some tangible recognition to demonstrate appreciation. A study by Morris Stein of industrial chemists asked them how they would like to be rewarded for developing a major product by rank-ordering twelve rewards. Those judged by colleagues to be most creative ranked a cash bonus significantly higher than those judged to be less creative. The latter preferred a paid trip to a scientific meeting; the other eleven rewards received almost identical rankings by the creative and less creative groups.[5] Social scientists, like their counterparts in the physical sciences, also need material rewards as positive signs of recognition of their worth to the organization.

> 5. *Do social scientists have the same or different feelings about their work, their colleagues, and their organizational superiors as do physical scientists in similar settings?*

In the chapter devoted to a comparison of attitudes of social scientists and physical scientists on similar questions affecting their work, the reader will recall that a majority of the social scientists were in positions of middle or top staff management, whereas most of the studies of physical scientists were conducted in research laboratories where they worked as "bench" scientists. The Pelz-Andrews study was the only one of any significance that separated Ph.D.'s from non-Ph.D.'s in the data presentation on scientists in industry. These two facts, taken together, undoubtedly affected the statistical results that were presented in Chapter 5. Nevertheless, it should be of interest to management to assess the attitude differences between social and physical scientists to eliminate or at least minimize the possibility of making unsound decisions affecting personnel policies for high-talent employees.

AUTONOMY

The assertions made by a number of writers that scientists in industry do not have enough autonomy does not hold for social scientists. As a matter of fact, the Pelz-Andrews study does not support such assertions for Ph.D. physical scientists.

COMMUNICATING IDEAS TO MANAGEMENT

Except for statisticians, neither the physical scientists nor the social scientists reflected difficulty in communicating new and important ideas to people in the organization who might be affected by them. However, there is strong indication that social scientists in research laboratories do have such difficulties even though their counterparts in the physical sciences in similar settings do not.

WORK INVOLVEMENT

Social scientists are more highly involved in their work than are physical scientists. Not fewer than half of the economists, psychologists, and sociologists indicated that they were very strongly or completely absorbed by their professional activities in the organizations where they worked, whereas this was true of only one in five of the physical scientists. The statisticians were about midway between the social scientists and physical scientists in their feelings about work involvement.

SELF-PERCEPTIONS OF IMPORTANCE OF THEIR WORK

Two-thirds of both the social scientists and physical scientists believe that they are making substantial contributions to their special fields. The sociologists were not quite as positive, although just under half of them had similar feelings.

ATTITUDES TOWARD ORGANIZATION RULES AND REGULATIONS

A large majority of scientists, regardless of fields of specialization, agree that professionals in industry resent and resist organization rules and regulations.

SUMMARY OF COMPARISON OF ATTITUDES BETWEEN SOCIAL SCIENTISTS AND PHYSICAL SCIENTISTS

In summary, it is clear that there are no significant differences in attitudes of social scientists as compared with physical scientists with respect to autonomy, communicating ideas to management, belief that their work is important, or general dislike of organization rules and regulations.

The major difference in attitude between social scientists and physical scientists is the feeling on the part of social scientists that they are more highly involved in their work.

The conclusion regarding differences is premised on the fact that scientists with doctorates, whether in the social or physical sciences, tend to regard their work perceptions similarly. There are no data to support or reject findings based on "scientists in industry" who do not have Ph.D.'s in their fields that are different from those which have been set forth here. We can, however, firmly support the statement by Pelz and Andrews that doctoral scientists are distinct unto themselves.

6. *A number of writers have stated that physical scientists in industry are more concerned about how they appear in the eyes of their fellow scientists in the profession than they are about their standing in the company. Simon Marcson has coined the phrase "colleague authority" to describe this feeling. Do social scientists exhibit similar attitudes toward colleague authority as do their physical science counterparts?*

Neither the data in this study nor comparative information obtained by Pelz and Andrews of Ph.D. physical scientists in industry support the widely held conclusion of a number of writers that professionals in private enterprise are very much concerned about colleague authority. In fact, colleagues outside of the organizations in which the respondents worked were ranked well below other persons or units who made judgments about their work. Economists and sociologists gave bottom ranking to professional colleagues elsewhere in their fields. Psychologists and statisticians were slightly more concerned about colleague authority, ranking professional colleagues third in a list of six possibilities. In the study by Pelz and Andrews, the Ph.D. physical scientists gave fourth rank to their colleagues outside of their organizations.

As to other persons or units that were ranked, we found a wide divergence in the attitudes shown toward top executives within the company. They were ranked first by economists and sociologists and at the bottom or next to the bottom by physical scientists, psychologists, and statisticians.

Physical scientists had a low opinion of the judgments of customers or non-technical departments that used their research. The ranking given to such persons or units was by far the lowest in their esteem. Social scientists, on the other hand, felt that some consideration should be given to the opinions of customers or non-technical departments when the work of the scientists was appraised.

All scientists place high value on the opinions of their work by their immediate organizational superiors. This was true regardless of field of science, level in the organization, or type of company.

IMPLICATION OF FINDINGS FOR APPRAISAL OF SCIENTISTS IN INDUSTRY

There is a strong correlation between the attitudes of economists and sociologists toward top executive appraisal of their work and the levels these social scientists occupy in their organizations. Because they are largely to be found in top staff positions, economists and sociologists are in much closer contact with the highest executives and are more fully involved in the decision-making processes in their organizations. If the other scientists were given opportunities to help top managers by drawing them into the discussions of central organization problems, it is very likely that their opinions toward the men in the highest ranks in the hierarchy would be more favorable. Of greater importance is the probability that their professional contributions would increase if they were called upon more directly.

One organization that has understood how to appraise a professional most effectively is Arthur D. Little, Inc., one of the world's largest and most eminent management consultant companies. This company employs about 600 professionals, two-thirds of whom hold doctorates in their fields. The vice-president for personnel was asked how the professionals in the organization were appraised. He explained in these words:

A professional put in charge of a client's problem is given the right to select any colleague of any rank in the company for his team providing that individual is available. This means that many of our senior people occupy dual roles: they administer departments or divisions and are also available to work as consultants for clients. Thus, a senior could be assigned to a junior if the latter asks for his services on a particular problem.

We do not use appraisal forms. Compensation and merit increases are determined by consultation between myself, the division or department head, and a member of top management. The appraisals come from clients. In some cases, however, it is possible for a client to be dissatisfied not because the judgements made by our man or men were faulty but for subjective reasons. Some recommendations, although of excellent professional quality, are not always acceptable to a client for a variety of reasons not connected with the professional's ability.

The approach used by this firm could be used by industry, both as to assignment of work and appraisal of professional performance. The "clients" in many cases would be the departments using the work of the social scientists. It can be seen that with this administrative approach, the social scientist would be much more concerned with his reputation internally than externally, that is, with higher executives, other departments using his work, and with clients, than with the opinions of colleagues outside of his organization.

7. *Do social scientists move about or do they settle down into careers in a particular company? If they have desires to leave their present positions, what kinds of opportunities would they look for in a new job?*

The number of jobs held since acquiring the Ph.D. is a good measure of the mobility or lack of it of social scientists now in industry. Are they job hoppers or do they settle down for a professional career in one organization? These data are important for our study for we need to know if highly trained professionals exhibit markedly different career patterns than those who are not specialists in private enterprise. The next two tables provide information on the questions raised here.

Number of Jobs Before Joining Present Organization and Field of Social Science

	Per cent			
Number of prior jobs	Econo- mists	Psychol- ogists	Sociol- ogists	Statis- ticians
None	26	18	22	45
1	40	37	28	40
2	21	32	28	0
3	9	8	10	10
4	2	5	6	5
5	2	0	6	0
	100	100	100	100
None, one or two jobs	87	87	78	85
Three or more jobs	13	13	22	15

The average American male, especially if he is a college graduate, usually works in two or three organizations before he finally settles down to finish out his career in one company. It is obvious from the table above that the majority of social scientists working full-time in industry do not make job changes very often during a normal lifetime career.

At a time when employment opportunities are plentiful for highly trained professionals, and the likelihood that this condition will obtain for the foreseeable future, it is of some significance that half or more of the respondents indicated fairly long service with one employer.

The two tables taken together indicate that social scientists in industry are not job hoppers and can be expected to seek long-time careers in one organization.

Years Served in Present Position and Field of Social Science

	Per cent			
Years	Econo-mists	Psychol-ogists	Sociol-ogists	Statis-ticians
up to 3	9	8	11	15
3 to 6	39	40	22	35
7 to 10	26	30	33	40
11 to 15	16	15	17	10
15 to 19	4	5	11	0
20 and over	6	2	6	0
	100	100	100	100
6 or less	48	48	33	50
7 or more	52	52	67	50

WHAT KINDS OF OPPORTUNITIES WOULD THEY LOOK FOR IN A NEW JOB?

We saw in the two tables above that social scientists by and large tend to stay in one organization when they find the conditions that attract them and hold their interest. There are times, no doubt, when every person is tempted by new possibilities or becomes restive or dissatisfied with his present situation. When that happens, the attractions of a new job would have to be strong enough to overcome resistance to change. What these attractions are and how they were ranked was set forth in Chapter 7. The most important considerations were given to opportunities to grow professionally, to work on difficult and challenging problems, to have considerable autonomy, and to be involved in the central problems of the organization. Pay was important too, but was ranked seventh in a list of eighteen considerations that would be given to a new job.

It should be noted that, except for statisticians who were located in research laboratories—where most of the companies were heavily involved in government contract work—that stability of employment was ranked last or almost last.

Some companies, in an effort to lure scientists by advertising visions of beaches or ski areas close to the locations of their work, or stressing "campus-like" atmosphere for their professionals obviously assume that such attractions are important for recruiting hard-to-get specialists. There was virtually no mention of a desire for idyllic surroundings by the respondents either in the interviews or write-in comments. A few complained about commuting and long hours, but none said that they preferred to work away from corporate headquarters "where the action is." Christopher Rand obviously did not interview social scientists in large organizations when he described the typical professional working in and around Cambridge, Massachusetts as "a scientist who likes a quiet office with a blackboard, a window, and a tree outside, and it is better still if the tree has a squirrel in it."[6]

As has been previously stated, pay *is* important; a prospective employer should not assume that competent social scientists will not give much attention to the size of the starting offer or to increases in salary later. At the same time, the evidence in this study clearly shows that high remuneration all by itself will not be enough to attract or hold professionals in private enterprise. In a discussion with the director of scientific personnel at the Brookhaven National Laboratory on the subject of recruitment and pay, he said that this non-profit organization has a waiting list of Ph.D. applicants who know that salary levels are much below those offered by corporate research laboratories. Brookhaven does no recruiting at college campuses and obtains all of its personnel requirements despite heavy competition from industry and rather bleak places to work in old barracks of Camp Yaphank of World War I days.

8. *Why do some social scientists leave industry? Would they be willing to accept another industrial position? If so, under what conditions or circumstances?*

The primary motivation for leaving industry expressed by those who left was the lack of opportunity to do important creative work for the organizations in which they were employed.

Lack of recognition was a second important force. The fact that the leavers were in much lower staff positions and were paid less than the stayers indicates either that those who left were not as highly regarded as those who stayed, or that their employers simply did not recognize the professional abilities of the leavers. In either case, it is difficult to obtain a true assessment in each situation. It should be remembered, however, that the largest number were offered and accepted positions as full professors, department chairmen, and deans in colleges and universities. Anyone who has been in both situations, knows that evaluations are based on different criteria. In academic life, the "publish or perish" syndrome is very much with us despite considerable lip service given to "teaching effectiveness." In order to be appointed to highest academic rank or to be considered for promotion if not at the level of full professor, the individual must produce a long list of published articles plus a book or two. If those social scientists who eventually left industry for academic life had this change in mind, they would have been concerned with how well they appeared in the eyes of professional colleagues outside of their companies, especially in colleges and universities by publishing in scholarly journals. Yet, lack of opportunities to publish was not an important source of dissatisfaction.

Over three-quarters of the respondents, when they were in industry, wanted opportunities to do important professional work and to get involved in other activities of the organization. Practically none of them wanted to move out of their special fields and into executive management.

A few of the leavers indicated some conflict between their personal goals and those of the organizations in which they worked. The number was not significant but cannot be totally discounted. It is not likely that such individuals will return to industrial positions.

Pelz and Andrews compared some data of stayers and leavers in a government organization. "They turned out to be similar in many respects, including colleague evaluation. One of the fears expressed was that better people were leaving; our data said not. But there was an interesting difference: those who left seemed to have a larger discrepancy between their organizational status and pay—and their evaluated level—than did those who stayed. In short, the leavers were under-recognized by the organization relative to achievement in the eyes of their colleagues," they wrote.[7]

WOULD THE LEAVERS BE WILLING TO ACCEPT ANOTHER INDUSTRIAL POSITION? IF SO, UNDER WHAT CONDITIONS OR CIRCUMSTANCES?

We saw from the data in Chapter 8 that at least half of those who left industry would like to return to positions in private enterprise. The reasons given by the respondents clearly indicated that intrinsic satisfactions—just as at the time of originally joining industry—were most important in their considerations. At the same time, extrinsic factors were also important, primarily as indicators of the individual's worth to the organization. Therefore, if one who had been in industry and left was approached by a company and an offer made, the management of that company would have to be prepared to demonstrate in positive ways in addition to size of the salary that the position would involve the social scientist in the highest professional sense.

IMPLICATIONS FOR THE DIRECTING FUNCTION OF MANAGEMENT

Those organizations who recognize the value of their professionals by giving considerable autonomy to social scientists to use their special skills to the fullest, involving them in central problems of the enterprise, and rewarding them extrinsically by higher status and better pay together with frequent contact with top executives, will have little difficulty in keeping highly trained professionals in their organizations. In general, the obverse can be assumed, that is, the lack of such attractions will provide the conditions for growing frustrations and eventual quitting to take positions that do provide opportunities for self-fulfillment.

The types of problems on which the social scientist is asked to work, the level of the people with whom he works, and recognition of his ability to make major contributions by using his ideas and suggestions, and giving him credit for them, should all add up to providing the kind of atmosphere in which professionals do their best work.

> 9. *How do social scientists react to the accusation made by Loren Baritz that they are merely paid servants of industrial management and willing to do its bidding even to the extent of distorting research findings in order to satisfy the desires of their employers?*

In any research that involves self-perceptions expressed by individuals in interviews or questionnaire replies, there is alway a problem of making judgments of the responses by the researcher. What he "hears" often depends on his background, personal views, and the kind of rapport he is able to establish with the respondents. The study presented here has been based almost entirely on opinions of the social scientists who consented to be interviewed or who returned completed questionnaires. When an individual holds an opinion, that opinion is a fact. One does not need to agree or disagree with the opinion in order to analyze responses quantitatively. Such use of the data avoids making value judgments. This study has presented opinions impartially both quantitatively and qualitatively.

A very wise professor, during a seminar for graduate students on how to undertake a research project, once said: "If you have the answer before you start your research, don't start." That admonition was carefully observed in this empirical study. There was no hypothesis to be proven or disproven. If the results seem to run counter to ideas held by others, it can only be said that there are data here to support the findings. This has not always been the case in some writings that are largely rhetorical or present views based on selected interviews that support the authors' beliefs.

There is no evidence in this study to support the assertion made by Baritz and others that social scientists in industry are willing to compromise or distort their findings to fit the desires of their employers. Although some of the respondents reported that they were under pressure to provide solutions to problems quickly, this kind of pressure is a source of dissatisfaction as we have already seen. If research data provided by the social scientists are misused, this happens in spite of warnings issued by them and not because of compliance on their part. If a time comes during the career of a highly trained individual when he believes that he is being used as a "stooge" by management, he leaves the organization.

The Typology of Social Scientists in Industry

After a social scientist has gained experience in the industrial world, he makes up his mind to follow one of three courses of action:

1. He will stay in his present organization because he has been given important problems to work on that challenge his professional ability and he has earned the esteem of his superiors, colleagues, and subordinates by the quality of his work as a scientist and a leader.

2. He will leave his present organization to look for another position in industry to satisfy his inward drive to be a professional in every sense of that word because he firmly believes that the private sector of our economy offers him the widest outlet for his special interest in a field for which he undertook long years of preparation.

3. He will leave private enterprise and not return to it because he has found that the industrial world does not provide him with the psychic satisfactions that he needs as a person and as a scientist.

The first two types might be called "industry-oriented social scientists"; the last, "academically oriented." Both types are needed in our pluralistic society to help solve the many complex problems that arise and to prepare future social scientists for fruitful and self-actualizing careers.

CONCLUSION

This study has been a probing journey into a relatively unexplored region—the world of the social scientist in industry. In this age of tremendous change, it is very likely that the social scientist is destined to play a major role in the industrial world. Private enterprise in its search for highly educated people to help organizations become as effective as possible will be trying to attract and hold competent professionals in industry. It is essential for good administration of high-talent manpower that this precious resource be utilized to its maximum capability. It is hoped that this study has provided valuable insights and will encourage future researchers to explore in more detail the world of work of the social scientist in industry.

BIBLIOGRAPHY

Abrahamson, Mark. "The Integration of Industrial Scientists," *Administrative Science Quarterly*, September, 1964.

Alexander, J. J. W.; Kemp, A. G.; and Rybczynski, T. M. (eds.). *The Economist in Business* (New York: Augustus M. Kelley, 1967).

American Psychological Association, The Division of Industrial Psychology. *The Psychologist in Industry* (Washington, D. C., 1959).

American Psychological Association, Education and Training Committee, Division 14. "Post Doctoral Training of Industrial Psychologists (Multilith report. P. 53) Washington, D. C., 1965.

Anthony, Robert N. *Management Control in Industrial Research* (Cambridge, Mass.: Graduate School of Business Administration, Harvard University, 1952).

Baritz, Loren. *The Servants of Power* (Middletown, Conn.: Wesleyan University Press, 1960).

Bass, Bernard M. and Vaughan, James A. *The Psychology of Learning for Managers* (New York: American Foundation for Management Research, 1965).

Berelson, Bernard (ed.). *The Behavorial Sciences Today* (New York: Basic Books, Inc., 1963).

Bogart, Leo. "Inside Marketing Research," *The Public Opinion Quarterly*, 27, (Winter 1963).

Bogart, Leo. "Use of Opinion Research," *Harvard Business Review*, March, 1951, pp. 113–124.

Bray, Douglas W. *Issues in the Study of Talent* (New York: King's Crown Press, 1954).

Brayfield, Arthur H., and Crockett, William H. "Employee Attitudes and Employee Performance," *Phychological Bulletin*, May, 1955.

Brown, J. Douglas. "A Climate for Discovery," in *Proceedings of a Conference on Academic and Industrial Basic Research* (Washington, D. C.: Government Printing Office, 1960).

Brown, Theodore H. "Improving the Tools of Business: Recent Literature on Mathematical Techniques," *Harvard Business Review,* Winter 1937.

Business Week. "The Man for All Seasons at C. B. S.," August 10, 1963.

Business Week. "Will Scientists Soon be a Surplus?" October 26, 1968, p. 81.

Butler, William F. "The Role of the Statistician in Policy Formulation," *Proceedings of the Business and Economics Statistics Association,* American Statistical Association, December, 1959.

Carlson, Robert O. "High Noon in the Research Marketplace," *The Public Opinion Quarterly,* 25 (Fall 1961).

Carlson, Robert O. untitled paper presented to the annual meeting of the American Sociological Association, (Mimeographed P. 13). August, 1962.

Chayes, Abram J. *The Corporation in Modern Society,* quoted in "The Intellectual's Challenge to the Corporate Executive," Public Opinion Index for Industry, September, 1961.

Clague, Ewan and Levine, Morton. "The Supply of Economists," *The American Economic Review,* May, 1962.

Danielson, Lee E. *Characteristics of Engineers and Scientists* (Ann Arbor: Bureau of Industrial Relations, University of Michigan, 1960).

Einstein, Albert. *Out of My Later Years* (New York: Philosophical Library, Inc., 1950).

Emerson, Harrington. *Efficiency as a Basis for Operation and Wages* (New York: The Engineering Magazine Publishing Company, 1911).

Feinberg, Morton R. and Lefkowitz, Jacob. "Image of Industrial Psychology Among Corporate Executives," *American Psychologist,* February, 1962.

Ferguson, Leonard W. "The Development of Industrial Psychology," in *Industrial Psychology,* B. von Haller Gilmer (ed.) (New York: McGraw-Hill Book Company, 1961).

Feuer, Lewis S. *The Scientific Intellectual* (New York: Basic Books, Inc., 1963).

Fitts, P. M. "Engineering Psychology," in *Psychology, A Study of a Science* (New York: McGraw-Hill Book Company, 1963), V.

Forbes. "Alter Egos: Paley and Stanton," January 15, 1964.

Galbraith, John K. *The New Industrial State* (Boston: Houghton Mifflin Company, 1967).

Gilmer, B. von Haller. *Industrial Psychology* (New York: McGraw-Hill Book Company, 1961).

Ginzberg, Eli. *The Development of Human Resources* (New York: McGraw-Hill Book Company, 1966).

Ginzberg, Eli and Herma, John L. *Talent and Performance* (New York: Columbia University Press, 1964) .

Ginzberg, Eli *et al. Occupational Choice* (New York: Columbia University Press, 1951).

Glaser, Barney G. *Organization Scientists* (New York: The Bobbs-Merrill Company, Inc., 1964).

Goldner, Fred H. "Role Emergence and the Ethics of Ambiguity," in *Ethics, Politics, and Social Research,* Gideon Sjoberg (ed.) (Cambridge, Mass.: Schenkman Publishing Company, Inc., 1967).

Gordon, Robert A. and Howell, James E. *Higher Education for Business* (New York: Columbia University Press, 1959).

Gouldner, Alvin W. "Cosmopolitans and Locals: Toward an Analysis of Latent Social Roles," *Administrative Science Quarterly*, December, 1957.

———. "Explorations in Applied Social Research," in *Marketing and the Behavorial Sciences*, Perry Bliss, (ed.) (Boston: Allyn & Bacon, Inc., 1963), pp. 4–24.

Hauser, Philip M. "Social Statistics, Social Science, and Social Engineering," *Proceedings of the Social Statistics Section*, American Statistical Association annual meeting, 1961.

Haworth, Leland. Statement before the U. S. sub-committee on the National Foundation for the Social Sciences, 90th Congress, 1967.

Hoadley, Walter E. Jr. "Statisticians Today and Tomorrow," *Journal of the American Statistical Association*, 54 (1) (1959).

Jaffe, Abraham J. and Adams, Walter. "College Education for U. S. Youth," *American Journal of Economics and Psychology*, April, 1964.

Johnson, Robert E. "Impact of Research and Development in the Electronics Industry," in *Proceedings of a Conference on Research and Development and Its Impact on the Economy*, National Science Foundation (Washington, D. C.: Government Printing Office, 1958).

Josephs, Devereux C. "Some Reflections on the Industry," *The American Behavorial Scientist*, May, 1963.

Kahn, Robert L. "Productivity and Job Satisfaction," *Personnel Psychology*, Autumn, 1960.

Kast, Fremont E. "Motivating the Organization Man," in *Management and Organizational Behavior Theories*, William T. Greenwood (ed.) (Cincinnati: South-Western Publishing Company, 1965).

Kornhauser, William. *Scientists in Industry: Conflict and Accommodation* (Berkeley: The University of California Press, 1962).

Krugman, Herbert E. "What Kind of Managers Will Scientists Make?" *Management Review*, May, 1958.

Kusch, Polykarp. *Columbia University Newsletter*, February 14, 1966.

Lancaster, Paul. "Handle With Care: Scientists in Industry Often Baffle the Bosses," *Wall Street Journal*, April 16, 1959.

Lazarsfeld, Paul F. "Sociological Reflections on Business," in *Social Science Research on Business: Product and Potential*, Robert A. Dahl, Mason Haire, and Paul F. Lazarsfeld (eds.) (New York: Columbia University Press, 1959).

Leeds, Ruth and Smith, Thomasino (eds.). *Using Social Science Knowledge in Business and Industry* (Ann Arbor: The Foundation for Research on Human Behavior and Richard D. Irwin, Inc., 1963).

Mahoney, Thomas A. "Managerial Perspectives of Organizational Effectiveness," *Management Science*, October, 1967.

Marcson, Simon. "Motivation and Productivity," in *Behavorial Science Research in Industrial Relations* (New York: Industrial Relations Counselors, 1962).

Marcson, Simon. "Report of Study of Social Science Research in U. S. Industry," (National Science Foundation, 1963), Unpublished.

Marcson, Simon. *The Scientist in American Industry* (Princeton: Industrial Relations Section, Princeton University, 1960).

Maslow, Abraham H. *Eupsychian Management* (Homewood, Ill.: Richard D. Irwin, Inc. and the Dorsey Press, 1965).

Massarik, Fred and Brown, Paula. "Social Research Faces Industry," *Personnel,* 30 (1954), 454–462.

May, Henry. *The Discontent of the Intellectuals: A Problem of the Twenties* (Chicago: Rand, McNally & Company, 1963).

McCabe, Rita. *American Women in Science and Engineering* (Cambridge, Mass.: M. I. T. Press, 1965).

McGregor, Douglas M. "An Uneasy Look at Performance Appraisal," *Harvard Business Review,* May–June, 1957.

Miller, Delbert C. "Industrial Sociology," *American Sociological Review,* 16 (1), 75–77.

Moore, Wilbert E. "Current Issues in Industrial Sociology," *American Sociological Review* (12) (December, 1947).

Moore, Wilbert E. "Industrial Sociology: Status and Prospects," *American Sociological Review* 13 (4).

National Academy of Sciences–National Research Council. *Doctorate Production in U. S. Universities 1920–1962* (Washington, D. C.: Government Printing Office, 1963).

National Academy of Sciences–National Research Council. *Profiles of Ph.D.'s in Sciences* (Washington, D. C.: National Academy of Sciences, 1965).

National Manpower Council. *A Policy for Scientific and Professional Personnel* (New York: Columbia University Press, 1953).

National Science Foundation. *American Science Manpower,* 1956 to 1968 (Washington, D. C.: Government Printing Office). These reports are published about one year after the dates shown in the title.

National Science Foundation. *Proceedings of a Conference on Research and Development and Its Impact on the Economy* (Washington, D. C.: Government Printing Office, 1958), p. 3.

New York Times. "Systems Analysts Are Baffled by Problems of Social Change," March 24, 1968.

Newman, Joseph W. "Put Research Into Marketing Decisions," *Harvard Business Review,* March–April, 1962, pp. 105–112.

Opinion Research Corporation. *The Conflict Between the Scientific Mind and the Management Mind* (Princeton: The Public Opinion Index for Industry, September, 1959).

Opinion Research Corporation. *The Intellectual's Challenge to the Corporate Executive* (Princeton: The Public Opinion Index for Industry, 1961).

Orth, Charles D.; Bailey, Joseph C.; and Wolek, Francis W. *Administering Research and Development* (Homewood, Ill.: Richard D. Irwin, Inc., and the Dorsey Press, 1964).

Pelz, Donald C. and Andrews, Frank M. *Scientists in Organizations* (New York: John Wiley & Sons, Inc., 1966).

Rand, Christopher. *Cambridge, U. S. A.* (New York: Oxford University Press, 1964).

Reirson, Roy L. "Response to Questionnaire on the Work of a Commercial Bank Economist," Paper prepared for the 5th International Conference of Commerical Bank Economists, (Mimeographed. 8 p.) June, 1956.

Roback, A. A. *et al. Present Day Psychology* (New York: Philosophical Library, Inc., 1955).

Roe, Anne. *The Making of a Scientist* (New York: Dodd, Mead and Company, 1952).

Roe, Anne. "A Psychologist Examines 64 Eminent Scientists," *Scientific American*, November, 1952.

Rogers, H. W. *Journal of Applied Psychology*, 1 (1917), 268–274.

Roman, Daniel D. *Research and Development Management* (New York: Appleton-Century-Crofts, 1968).

Scott, W. D. "Scientific Selection of Salesmen," *Advertising and Selling*, 5, 6, and 7 (1915).

Schultz, George P. and Whisler, Thomas L. *Management Organization and the Computer* (New York: The Free Press, 1965).

Shepard, Herbert A. "Nine Dilemmas in Industrial Research," *Administrative Science Quarterly*, December, 1956.

Sielaff, T. J. (ed.). *Statistics in Action* (San Jose, California: The Lansford Press, 1963).

Silk, Leonard S. *The Research Revolution* (New York: McGraw-Hill Book Company, 1960).

Snider, Joseph L. (ed.). "Symposium on the Industrial Economist," *Harvard Business Review*, 20 (3), 1942.

Snow, Charles P. *Two Cultures: and a Second Look* (London: Cambridge University Press, 1963).

Stein, Morris I. "Creativity and the Scientist," in *The Sociology of Science*, Bernard Barber and Walter Hirsch (eds.) (New York: Free Press of Glencoe, 1962).

Stouffer, Samuel A. "Methods of Research Used by American Social Scientists," in *The Behavorial Sciences Today*, Bernard Berelson, (ed.) (New York: Basic Books, Inc., 1963).

Teitsworth, Clark S. "Growing Role of the Company Economists," *Harvard Business Review*, January–February, 1959.

Terman, Lewis M. "Are Scientists Different?" *Scientific American*, January, 1955.

Thorndike, Robert L. and Hagen, Elizabeth. *Ten Thousand Careers* (New York: John Wiley and Sons, Inc., 1959).

Tiffin, Joseph. "How Psychologists Serve Industry," *Personnel Journal*, March, 1958.

Viteles, Morris S. *Industrial Psychology* (New York: W. W. Norton & Company, Inc., 1932).

Weiner, Norbert A. "A Rebellious Scientist After Two Years," *Bulletin of the Atomic Sciences*, November, 1948.

Wilkinson, John. "The Quantitative Society or What Are You to Do With the Noodle?" An Occasional Paper of the Center for the Study of Democratic Institutions, Santa Barbara, California, 1965.

Whyte, William F. "Applying Behavorial Science Research to Management Problems," in *Social Science Approaches to Business Behavior*, George Strother (ed.) (Homewood, Ill.: Dorsey Press and Richard D. Irwin, Inc., 1962).

Wolfle, Dael. "Supply of Scientific Manpower," *Proceedings of the Second Conference on Scientific Manpower*, National Science Foundation (Washington, D. C.: Government Printing Office, 1952).

Zander, Alvin. "Resistance to Change: Its Analysis and Prevention," *Advanced Management*, January, 1950.

NOTES

1. INTRODUCTION

1. John K. Galbraith, *The New Industrial State,* p. 73.
2. Harrington Emerson, *Efficiency as a Basis for Operation and Wages,* p. 131.
3. Statement of Leland Haworth before the U.S. Senate subcommittee on the National Foundation for the Social Sciences, 90th Congress, 1967.
4. Donald C. Pelz and Frank M. Andrews, *Scientists in Organizations.*
5. Charles D. Orth, Joseph C. Bailey, and Francis W. Wolek, *Administering Research and Development,* p. 4.
6. Dael Wolfle, "Supply of Scientific Manpower," *Proceedings of the Second Conference on Scientific Manpower,* National Science Foundation, 1952.
7. Ewan Clague and Morton Levine, "The Supply of Economists," pp. 497–502.
8. *American Science Manpower 1968,* a Report of the National Register of Scientific and Technical Personnel (Washington: National Science Foundation, 1969).
9. Simon Marcson, *The Scientist in American Industry.*
10. Loren Baritz, *The Servants of Power.*

2. THE ROLE OF THE SOCIAL SCIENTIST IN INDUSTRY

1. See especially, American Psychological Association, *The Psychologist in Industry;* William F. Butler, "The Role of the Statistician in Policy Formulation"; Leonard W. Ferguson, "The Development of Industrial Psychology"; Barney G. Glaser, *Organization Scientists.* (The title is somewhat misleading; this is a case study of scientists within one government medical research

organization.); Fred H. Goldner, "Role Emergence and the Ethics of Ambiguity"; Fred Massarik and Paula Brown, "Social Research Faces Industry"; Delbert C. Miller, "Industrial Sociology"; Wilbert E. Moore, "Industrial Sociology: Status and Prospects"; George P. Schultz and Thomas L. Whisler, *Management Organization and the Computer*; Clark S. Teitsworth, "Growing Role of the Company Economist"; Joseph Tiffin, "How Psychologists Serve Industry." A book based on the role of the economist in British enterprises has many chapters that probably apply to American business economists: J. J. W. Alexander, A. G. Kemp, and T. M. Rybczynski (eds.), *The Economist in Business.*

2. Simon Marcson, "Report of Study of Social Science Research in U.S. Industry," National Science Foundation.
3. Joseph L. Snider, ed., "Symposium on the Industrial Economist."
4. Clark S. Teitsworth, "Growing Role of the Company Economist," pp. 97–104.
5. Roy L. Reirson, "Response to Questionnaire on the Work of a Commercial Bank Economist."
6. Robert E. Johnson, "Impact of Research and Development in the Electronics Industry," pp. 33–41.
7. *Business Week,* "The Man for All Seasons at CBS."
8. Morris S. Viteles, *Industrial Psychology.* Viteles cited the pioneering work of Scott in salesmen selection (W.D. Scott, "Scientific Selection of Salesmen," *Advertising and Selling,* 5, 6, and 7 (1915); and an investigation of the use of tests for clerical personnel (H.W. Rogers, *Journal of Applied Psychology,* 1 (1917), 268–274.)
9. A. A. Roback, *et al., Present Day Psychology,* p. 428.
10. Rita McCabe of I.B.M., a panelist at an M.I.T. symposium gave the conferees this definition. The meeting was published under the title *American Women in Science and Engineering.* See pp. 25–26.
11. Morton R. Feinberg and Jacob Lefkowitz, "Image of Industrial Psychology Among Corporate Executives," pp. 109–111.
12. American Psychological Association, "Post Doctoral Training of Industrial Psychologists." The writer was a member of this committee.
13. Bernard Berelson (ed.), *The Behavorial Sciences Today,* p. 235.
14. Robert O. Carlson, untitled paper presented at the annual meeting of the American Sociological Association, Aug. 1962.
15. Leo Bogart, "Inside Marketing Research," pp. 562–577, and "Use of Opinion Research," pp. 113–124.
16. Simon Marcson, *The Scientist in American Industry,* p. 19.
17. Joseph W. Newman, "Put Research Into Marketing Decisions."
18. Theodore H. Brown, "Improving the Tools of Business," pp. 253–260.
19. Walter E. Hoadley, Jr., "Statisticians Today and Tomorrow," pp. 1–11.
20. William F. Butler, "The Role of the Statistician in Policy Formulation," p. 314.
21. National Science Foundation, *Proceedings of a Conference on Research and Development,* p. 3.
22. American Psychological Association, *The Phychologist in Industry.*
23. B. von Haller Gilmer, *Industrial Psychology,* p. 4.

24. Quoted in a weekly newsletter sent to executives from the Employee Relations Department of Standard Oil Company (New Jersey) to all its affiliates.
25. Thomas A. Mahoney, "Managerial *Perspectives* of Organizational Effectiveness," pp. 8, 76–91.
26. P. M. Fitts, "Engineering Psychology," pp. 909, 932.
27. *New York Times*, "Systems Analysts are Baffled by Problems of Social Change."
28. Bernard M. Bass and James A. Vaughan, *The Psychology of Learning for Managers*, p. 13.
29. Robert O. Carlson, "High Noon in the Research Marketplace."
30. Alvin W. Gouldner, "Explorations in Applied Social Research," pp. 4, 24.
31. Devereux C. Josephs, "Some Reflections on the Industry," p. 5.
32. Philip M. Hauser, "Social Statistics, Social Science, and Social Engineering," p. 181.
33. T. J. Sielaff, (ed.), "The Occupational Outlook for Statisticians," pp. 247–251.

3. FACTORS IN THE CAREER SELECTIONS OF SOCIAL SCIENTISTS IN INDUSTRY

1. Eli Ginzberg, *et al., Occupational Choice*, p. 17.
2. Robert L. Thorndike and Elizabeth Hagen, *Ten Thousand Careers*, p. 50.
3. Eli Ginzberg, *The Development of Human Resources*, p. 56.
4. Douglas W. Bray, *Issues in the Study of Talent*, p. 45.
5. Abraham J. Jaffee and Walter Adams, "College Education for U.S. Youth," p. 274.
6. Anne Roe, *The Making of a Scientist*, pp. 21–25.
7. Eli Ginzberg and John L. Herma, *Talent and Performance*.
8. National Academy of Sciences–National Research Council, *Doctorate Production in U.S. Univeristies 1920–1961*.

4. WHY SOCIAL SCIENTISTS ACCEPT POSITIONS IN INDUSTRY

1. William Kornhauser, *Scientists in Industry: Conflict and Accommodation*.

5. ATTITUDES OF INDUSTRIAL SOCIAL SCIENTISTS TOWARD THEIR WORK: COMPARISON WITH ATTITUDES OF PHYSICAL SCIENTISTS IN INDUSTRY

1. Charles P. Snow, *Two Cultures: and a Second Look*, pp. 69–70.
2. Lewis M. Terman, "Are Scientists Different?" pp. 25–29.
3. Anne Roe, "A Psychologist Examines 64 Eminent Scientists," pp. 21–25.
4. Robert A. Anthony, *Management Control in Industrial Research*, p. 31.

5. Paul Lancaster, "Handle With Care: Scientists in Industry Often Baffle the Bosses," p. 1.
6. Mark Abrahamson, "The Integration of Industrial Scientists," pp. 208–218.
7. Simon Marcson, *The Scientist in American Industry*, p. 129 and "Motivation and Productivity," p. 163.
8. Robert N. Anthony, *Management Control in Industrial Research Organizations*, p. 53.
9. Opinion Research Corporation, The Public Opinion Index for Industry, *The Conflict Between the Scientific Mind and the Management Mind*, p. 16.
10. Fremont E. Kast, "Motivating the Organization Man," p. 793.
11. Ruth Leeds and Thomasina Smith, eds., *Using Social Science Knowledge in Business and Industry*, pp. 14–15.
12. Opinion Research Corporation, *The Conflict Between the Scientific Mind and the Management Mind;* Lee E. Danielson, *Characteristics of Engineers and Scientists;* Simon Marcson, *The Scientist in American Industry;* William Kornhauser, *Scientists in Industry*.
13. Robert N. Anthony, *Management Control in Industrial Research*, p. 31.
14. Wilbert E. Moore, "Current Issues in Industrial Sociology," pp. 651–657.
15. Loren Baritz, *The Servants of Power*, p. 198.
16. Norbert A. Weiner, "A Rebellious Scientists After Two Years."
17. Lewis S. Feuer, *The Scientific Intellectual*, p. 12.
18. Abram J. Chayes, *The Corporation in Modern Society*.
19. Douglas M. McGregor, "An Uneasy Look at Performance Appraisal," pp. 89–94.
20. Leonard S. Silk, *The Research Revolution*, p. 119.
21. Alvin W. Gouldner, "Cosmopolitans and Locals: Toward an Analysis of Latent Social Roles," pp. 4–24.
22. Donald C. Pelz and Frank M. Andrews, *Scientists in Organizations*, pp. 3, 4.
23. Paul Lancaster, "Handle With Care," p. 1.
24. Donald C. Pelz and Frank M. Andrews, *Scientists in Organizations*, pp. 21–22.

6. SATISFACTIONS AND DISSATISFACTIONS OF SOCIAL SCIENTISTS IN INDUSTRY

1. Eli Ginzberg and John L. Herma, *Talent and Performance*, p. 138.
2. Arthur H. Brayfield and William H. Crockett, "Employee Attitudes and Employee Performance," pp. 396–422.
3. See especially Robert L. Kahn, "Productivity and Job Satisfaction," pp. 275–281.
4. Herbert A. Shepard, "Nine Dilemmas in Industrial Research," pp. 295–309.
5. Alvin Zander, "Resistance to Change: Its Analysis and Prevention," pp. 9–11.
6. Robert O. Carlson, of the Standard Oil Company (New Jersey), untitled paper dated August, 1962.

7. How Social Scientists in Industry See Their Future Careers

1. *Forbes*, "Alter Egos: Paley and Stanton."
2. Herbert E. Krugman, "What Kind of Managers Will Scientists Make?" pp. 22–28.
3. John Wilkinson, "The Quantitative Society or What Are You to Do With the Noodle?" p. 3.
4. National Manpower Council, *A Policy for Scientific and Professional Manpower*, p. 255.
5. Abraham H. Maslow, *Eupsychian Management*, pp. 192–193.
6. Henry May, *The Discontent of the Intellectuals: A Problem of the Twenties*, p. 9.
7. Professor Polykarp Kusch quoted in the *Columbia University Newsletter* of February 14, 1966.
8. Anne Roe, *The Making of a Scientist*, p. 232.
9. Albert Einstein, *Out of My Later Years*, p. 113.
10. William F. Whyte, "Applying Behavorial Science Research to Management Problems," pp. 125–140.
11. Samuel A. Stouffer, "Methods of Research Used by American Social Scientists," p. 67.
12. Robert A. Gordon and James E. Howell, *Higher Education for Business*, pp. 166–167.
13. Wilbert E. Moore, "Current Issues in Industrial Sociology," pp. 382–400.
14. National Academy of Sciences–National Research Council, *Profiles of Ph.D.s in Sciences*, p. 15.

8. Why Some Social Scientists Leave Industry

1. Fred H. Goldner, "Role Emergence and the Ethics of Ambiguity," pp. 245–266.
2. Daniel D. Roman, *Research and Development Management*, p. 27.
3. *Business Week*, "Will Scientists Soon Be a Surplus?" p. 81.

9. Summary of Major Findings: Implications for Management

1. Paul F. Lazarsfeld, "Sociological Reflections on Business," p. 101.
2. J. Douglas Brown, "A Climate for Discovery," pp. 66–68.
3. National Science Foundation, *American Science Manpower 1968*, 1969.
4. Donald C. Pelz and Frank M. Andrews, *Scientists in Organizations*, pp. 125–126.
5. Morris I. Stein, "Creativity and the Scientist," pp. 329–343.
6. Christopher Rand, *Cambridge, U. S. A.*, p. 9.
7. Donald C. Pelz and Frank M. Andrews, *Scientists in Organizations*, p. 111.

INDEX

This book was set in Baskerville Linotype and printed by letterpress on P & S Old Forge manufactured by P. H. Glatfelter Co., Spring Grove, Pa. Composed, printed and bound by H. Wolff Book Manufacturing Company Inc., New York, N. Y.